Running Red

One red horse, two Alaskan girls, many dangers . . .

KATIE HALLEY

Since 1978

PO Box 221974 Anchorage, Alaska 99522-1974
books@publicationconsultants.com
www.publicationconsultants.com

ISBN 978-1-59433-163-3
ebook 978-1-59433-166-4
Library of Congress Catalog Card Number: 2010938950

Manufactured in the United States of America

Dedication

This book is dedicated to Nana, who always believed in me.

Katie Halley

Prologue

The baby blue sky became dark and the stars began to twinkle. It was a night of no moon, and the stone figure of a horse was barely visible. A mare, with a coat as red as the desert sun, approached it. Her rock-hard hooves made a slight echo on the mountain. Her eyes were full of worry, but a hint of joy remained. She raised her noble head to the sky and shouted, "Sunrise, reveal!"

The words seemed to spread for miles around, and then it came back to her ears like a boomerang. A bright, golden light appeared from the stone and it shook violently. As the stone figure cracked apart, a rearing stallion appeared before the mare. He shone with the glow of a fresh new morning light, and his piercing black eyes were knowing and warm.

"Red Mare!" boomed a voice, "You have summoned me."

The glowing stallion stood majestically before her. He was golden, like the summer sun, and shone with a light that was almost transparent. His hooves were ten times harder than any diamond, and a sparkling mist hovered around him.

The mare bowed her head respectfully, "Sunrise, I have seen a disturbing picture through the Dream Pool."

The stallion squinted. "Go on."

Red Mare lifted her beautiful head, "A child has been stolen, sir, by the Toblins."

"Tell me more."

The mare nodded. "I saw a young girl, the age of five. She was playing in the woods when they found her and took her away."

"What did the child look like?"

"She had blond hair and ice-blue eyes."

"Does she have a sibling?"

"Yes, Your Grace. They were playing together at the time."

"Hmm, the prophecy is unfolding; your time here is almost at a close."

"Wait! Please! Let me rescue the girl first and send her home. Please, I can't leave yet! I can be done within days, maybe hours! It's too dangerous for her. Please let me do this!"

"No!" his voice boomed so loud that the mare fell to her knees.

"You know the prophecy, Red Mare! The sibling must rescue her, and then you must finish your journey. It is your destiny, and you must fulfill it. I will permit you to help the sibling until you reach Mount Frost. You will then come back here for your ... departure."

As she bowed her head in acceptance, a tear began to roll down the mare's cheek. Before it hit the ground, Sunrise caught it. "Do not cry, for if your tears hit the ground, your home will be destroyed."

Red Mare's shoulders slumped wearily as Sunrise lay down and turned back into stone.

Chapter 1

Fall in Talkeetna, Alaska is beautiful. The sun was sending golden rays through the green and gold leaves of the birch trees. Dapples of light and shadows covered the underbrush. Berries that grew in abundance were starting to dwindle after many children, birds and bears spent the summer filling their stomachs with the sweet fruit. Birds sang as soloists and as a choir, and every once in a while a fox or moose would betray their noble presence.

Annie was happy to see termination dust on the lower mountains. When this first dusting of snow returned to the peaks, it signified the time when the tourists were gone and the night sky returned. She loved gazing at Denali on a clear day and watching the northern lights on a clear night. She knew in her heart she lived in one of the prettiest places on the planet. But Annie didn't feel happy or content that night.

She cradled a small red toy horse Nana gave her before she passed away. She wanted to cry but held back the tears. Earlier that evening her parents told her to control herself and stop crying. She found it hard to do because her sister disappeared earlier that day. She thought back to that afternoon when they were playing in the trees and frolicking in the meadow. The fireweed had turned to cotton and the first chill of fall raised goosebumps.

Then they heard a snakelike voice say, "Get her."

Frightened, they ran back to the house. Annie got there first because she was faster. Louise never showed up. The snake voices took her little sister.

"I'm eight years old; I should've protected her! I should have done something!" she wailed to herself. She looked at the empty bed across the room with watery eyes and saw her reflection in the mirror on the other side of the room. She had long, straight, brown hair with ice-blue sad eyes. *What happened to Louise? I should have been the one to get caught.*

Down the hall, she could hear her parents snoring and sleeping peacefully. Dad spent the day chopping wood for the winter, and mom put up jars of fireweed jelly and blueberry jam. Neither appeared worried and reminded Annie that Louise had pulled stunts like this before and had always shown up eventually, bragging of imaginative adventures. They lived in such a close knit town that they always felt safe. Dad had shown them both how to live off the land and how to use a knife in an emergency.

That afternoon Louise only had a small pocket knife attached to her belt.

You'd think they'd be up all night worrying and trying to find her. They just went to bed like nothing happened! That's not right. They didn't hear the voices! They think I'm just being dramatic.

She looked at her clock and it read 12:59 a.m. She couldn't get to sleep. Her worried mind wouldn't let her. Quietly getting out of bed, she tiptoed over to her bookcase and read some of the familiar titles. She had a large vocabulary for her age and she knew how to read fifth-grade-level books. Her favorite series was *The Chronicles of Narnia* by C.S. Lewis; but this time she reached for a book she had written herself. It was titled *The Misty Garden Horses.* To her it was the best horse book ever. Her sister had asked her to read it to her over and over, but this time she would have to read it to herself.

Annie walked to the bed with her book and picked up the red horse. She set it down next to her and began to read when she heard a voice say, "Put down the book."

A sudden rush of fear pulsed through her. She looked up to her doorway but no one was there. She turned to the window. Nobody.

"Who are you?" she whispered to the voice.

"A friend. Now listen to me, as we don't have much time. Take the little horse and climb out your window."

"Climb out my window?" Annie whispered in surprise, "Why?"

"You're on the ground floor. Now climb out!"

"But I don't know you! I'm afraid."

"Trust me," the voice said urgently, "I'm here to help you find your sister."

That did it. All she wanted to do was find her sister, so she got out of bed and opened the window. Stepping out, she saw that the forest was only a few feet away, and every shadow looked eerie. The grass was cool and slick on her bare feet and she heard a rustling in the darkness.

"Set the horse down in the grass. Make sure it is standing, please."

She did as she was told and set the toy down. It began to turn a deeper red and a white light engulfed it. She gasped as it grew into a real horse. The mare was red like the desert sun, and her mane and tail swayed like red reeds.

"Who are you?"

Gently lifting her noble head, the horse turned to face the girl. "I'm…"

But her words were cut off by a voice like a snake's, "Sssssss-ccchild, ssssssweeeee areshhhhhere tooo hhhelp."

"Annie, get on my back," the horse ordered.

The girl was frozen in fear as a shape wriggled from the devil's club. It didn't have any back legs, but slithered around on its tail like a snake. It had two arms, each with three clawed fingers. Its head was goblin-like, though its large, round, yellow eyes had slit pupils like a serpent's.

"Annie, now!" the mare ordered.

Ten more creatures sneaked from the bushes and slowly

crept toward them. The red mare sounded desperate as she whinnied into Annie's ear, "Now!"

Annie broke out of her trance and climbed upon the mare's back. The mare kicked away a Toblin trying to grab her leg as they galloped off into the forest. The girl didn't have a hard time staying on because she had a horse of her own. She had been riding for years, even before she could walk. Glancing behind her, she saw the creatures storming after them. As the trees thinned, horse and girl approached the meadow were Annie and Louise had been playing earlier that day.

The horse tensed and whinnied, "Four Hooves, open!"

A blinding white circle appeared before them, making Annie blink rapidly. She could have sworn that she saw three horses standing side by side, like statues of light. A Toblin screeched and grabbed hold of the mare's back legs. The red mare tripped forward and thrashed, but couldn't kick the Toblin off. More of the creatures approached and tried to grasp onto her other legs. Annie screamed and kicked at the creatures' faces, which caused them to turn their attention to her and attempt to drag her down.

"Help!" she screamed.

The girl, looking toward the portal, could once again see the outline of the horses. All three opened their eyes and reared, leaving the portal to boldly gallop around the Toblins. Annie managed to kick off a few of the creatures and pulled herself back upon the mare's back. The sight of the lighted horses distracted them, giving Red and Annie the chance they needed.

"Hold on," the red horse instructed as she jumped over the Toblins and into the gleaming white portal. Everything went black.

———

Annie looked up from where she was lying. A lush green forest was all around her. Her head rested against a large root poking out of the ground, and an old oak shaded her from the rising sun. *That's strange*, she thought, *we don't have oak trees in Alaska.* She shook her head and sat up, feeling a little dizzy. The red mare stood with her back to the girl, her noble head low. Annie got to her feet and walked a little unsteadily to her. "What just happened?"

The horse sighed, "Those creatures are called Toblins. They serve a distant monster that lives high on the slopes of Mount Frost."

"What about that portal, and the three white horses? Who are they and where am I? Why didn't I stay awake through the passing?"

"I cannot tell you about the horses. You'll know when the time is right. A human passing from one world to the next can never remember the experience. Something about the force of it makes them black out."

She considered this for a moment and then asked, "Why are you helping me find my sister? How did you know she was missing?"

"That I can't tell you at this time, it's too complicated. She paused and then said, "Come on now. We have till the full moon. Get on my back."

Annie climbed on and wiped the dirt from her pajamas. "Will I be able to change into something more suitable for riding?"

The mare snorted and walked onward, moving quickly into a brisk canter. The sun beat down on them as they glided through the forest.

Human and horse, Annie thought, *the perfect combination.* The wind whipped around her hair and over her face. Birds sang and squirrels chattered as they jumped through the trees. They passed over many streams and fallen trees, gliding over them as if they had wings. A brown stag stared quietly at them as they passed, and foxes ran along their side for a minute or two.

"What is your name? I don't know what to call you."

The horse snorted again and waved her mane, "If you must know, my name is Red Mare."

Annie rode in silence for a while. *Red Mare? Not a very complicated name. I like it.*

Red Mare slowed to a trot, then to a full stop. "You need a break," she said.

The girl knew it was really the horse needing the break, as she was breathing heavily and her chest and back were damp with sweat. The bushes surrounding them held a purple fruit that looked larger than a plum but smaller than an apple. It smelled spicy.

"What kind of fruit is that? It looks yummy."

"That is a very dangerous fruit and you need to stay away from it," replied Red Mare. "Anybody who touches or eats it falls into a deep sleep. No one can wake from it except in a time of great need."

Annie shivered and backed away, afraid of falling into one of the bushes and squishing the fruit with her hand. Looking skyward, Annie guessed it was close to noon. *No wonder her stomach was growling,* she thought.

Red Mare raised her head and sniffed the air, "Come. Arfag Town is just ahead."

"Arfag? What kind of place is that?"

"Never mind. Just get on my back."

Arfag Town loomed in the distance. As they approached, Annie noticed many tents and tables lining the street. Stables and small grocery stores stood on either side. Many houses and huts dotted the town and most had barns and gardens. Some had corrals where cattle and horses were kept. The smell of cooking fires, spices, and manure filled the air.

Red Mare trotted onward and stopped where a dirt road began. A sign beside the road boasted in big black letters **Welcome to Arfag**. The girl and horse walked through crowds of people buying and selling. Annie felt hot with embarrassment when most of the people stopped and stared at her.

They came to the front of a large building with a stable. The front door was wooden and looked like you'd have a handful of splinters if you knocked. The yard was overgrown with weeds. A little sign above the door said, 'Arfag Inn, Best in the World!'

"Get off and check in," Red Mare ordered.

"I don't have any money. Won't it cost something?"

"Not when they see me."

Annie slipped off the mare's back and walked toward the door. As she knocked, a man quickly opened the door before she had finished. Once again she felt a wave of embarrassment, as the man looked her over. He was chubby and wore a green and blue suit—it seemed from another century, perhaps from the fifteen hundreds.

"May I, uhm, help you, Miss?"

"Yes, I'd like to check in, me and my horse."

He looked behind her and suddenly his eyes grew wide. "Oh my, Milady! You've stopped at my inn? What an honor!"

Red Mare nodded and snorted, "Get some clothes for my companion. We were robbed and left with nothing."

"Yes, oh yes! I'll be right back!"

Annie turned to the mare when the man went back inside. "What was that all about?"

"Why do you ask so many questions?"

"I want to know what's going on! Why are you keeping secrets from me?"

"Fine," said the mare. "I'm what you would call a magic horse. That's the simplest way to explain. I'm well known and very well respected."

"Why don't you tell me everything?" Annie beseeched her.

"It's not that I'm withholding from you. There are simply too many eyes and ears around here. Besides, the less you know, the better off you'll be."

The girl looked at her, very confused. Obviously, Red Mare wasn't going to answer any further questions at the moment.

The man rushed back with a neat little box. He handed it, along with a key, to Annie. "There you are Milady, room ten upstairs."

Annie accepted the box and key and looked back at the mare. "What about Red …." The horse shot her a look of pure warning, "I mean my horse. Where will she go?"

"I've already sent stable hands to clean stable number one. She'll be well cared for. Don't worry, Miss."

Annie said goodbye to the horse and walked into the inn. It was decent inside with tapestries and paintings of horses on the walls. It smelled of ale and grease.

The innkeeper accompanied her to the stairs. "Room ten is up there." He pointed a round, pudgy finger at the second floor. There were ten rooms in all with a number in fancy script on each wooden door.

"May I ask you a question?" said Annie.

"Yes, Miss."

"What is your name? Or should I just call you innkeeper?"

"My name is Mr. Beeter," he answered, giving a polite bow. "At your service."

His bow made her laugh a little and she answered, "My name is Amy," she said with a slight a curtsy. She didn't want to lie to Mr. Beeter, but Red Mare seemed to stress that they use different names.

"Mr. Beeter, do you have books that I could browse through to pass the time? Maybe something about the history of your town?"

Sadness suddenly filled his big brown eyes. "No, not here in Arfag." His voice dropped to a whisper. "There hasn't been a book here since they have taken over. They're all around, listening, watching. Everyone here is under their control except for me, of course."

Fear bit at her gut. *They? Who are they?* A haunting feeling crept up her spine and into her brain. The comforting inn now felt like a haunted house in which she would be doomed forever.

"Oh dear, I'm sorry to scare you, Miss Amy. You best beware coming into town on a mare like that. She's special, that one. They'll be attracted to her power."

"I don't know much about the horse. She doesn't like to talk much."

Mr. Beeter nodded with understanding. "Yes, I know. Those horses are powerful, but they don't like to speak in public. It would be too dangerous."

"Well, Mr. Beeter, I must get out of these clothes. Before I go, do you know of any place where I can get a look at any of those forbidden books?"

"Yes, I do, but I can't talk about it out here. We'll talk later."

Room ten was very cozy, though it reminded her of home and her sister. A wave of sadness washed over her; she missed her parents and wanted to be back there right now. She longed to sit on her sister's bed and read her stories. She wanted to tuck her in and then wake up and go play in their backyard forest. Now Louise was gone, and Annie was in some strange world far from home. Her parents must be frantic! At least, she hoped they were.

She slowly opened the box that Mr. Beeter had given her. Inside, she saw a thin, creamy brown shirt. A leather vest lay under it, along with a more comfortable version of English riding britches. They looked old-fashioned and sturdy. She also pulled out a dark green and brown skirt that matched her shirt.

How nice of him to include all these clothes!

Annie slipped on the pants and shirt, and folded the vest, pajamas, and skirt. Then she placed them back into the box and went downstairs.

Chapter 2

Annie looked out the window of her room. The town's activity had died down, but a few people still walked along the streets. She smiled when a few younger girls ran after each other, squealing playfully. A teenage girl rode on her dusty mare down the street and into the field. The girl looked up at Annie as if she knew her. She made eye contact and then quickly looked away. Annie saw that the horse the girl was riding was strong and glowed with the health that only a caring, devoted master could bestow. In the distance rose mist-covered mountains, glowing in the setting sun.

I wish this were my home, and then my family would be right here with me.

A knock upon the door startled Annie from her thoughts. "Come in."

Mr. Beeter opened the door just wide enough to poke his head in. "Miss Amy? You might want to come see this," he whispered.

He led her down the hallway, pausing to look over the railing to see if anyone was watching. He stopped at a bookcase filled with paintings and small woven things. Mr. Beeter took out a set of keys and moved a fairly large painting over and placed the key downward. Annie was surprised to see it go down. Turning the key, Mr. Beeter pushed the bookcase inward. It moved silently and he slipped in. Annie followed and closed the case behind her. The innkeeper lit candles, thus spreading a warm glow across the room. A larger bookcase sat against the wall—this one was stuffed with books! Annie grinned and ran.

"Oh, this is wonderful!" she exclaimed. "I thought you said you didn't have any books!"

"I didn't want them to hear me. They're already looking for you."

"Me?"

"Some man asked if I had seen a small girl wandering around alone in the inn. I told him you had gone out shopping in the marketplace."

Fear and relief washed over Annie like an ocean wave. "They wanted *me*?"

He nodded gravely, "I'd lock my door tonight, Miss."

Annie shivered, then turned to look at the books. There were many of them, but none of them had titles she recognized. Rather, there were titles such as, *The Eyes of Mt. Ablaze, The Siege of Shadows, The Dark Wolf,* and *The Crooked Tree.* Annie's small finger scanned the leather covers. So many books—books nobody on earth had ever read! One book in particular caught her eye; it was one of the thicker volumes, entitled *Galloping Across Fire.* Annie pulled it out and ran her hand over the cover. The title was inscribed with ink and it had a picture of a horse galloping over flames.

"What's this book about?"

"That book is one of the books most sought after by them. It tells how the legends started and the history of our world. The book you are holding is about horses and magic and is a noble book. Read that, my girl, and the knowledge it gives you will be your biggest weapon."

"May I keep it and start reading it tonight?"

"Yes, but keep it hidden. Have your door locked and your window curtains drawn."

"Yes Sir," Annie said, holding it close to her chest and looking around her cautiously.

———•———

Annie entered the stables. The walls and ground were golden, lit by the last rays of the sun. Red Mare was standing and half dozing. She blinked at Annie while alertness came back into her eyes.

"I just wanted to check how you were doing, Red."

The mare flicked her ears, "I am well. You better get to sleep. I expect us to leave sometime before the sun reaches its highest point."

Annie nodded and turned around feeling dismissed. *That mare doesn't really care about me. She acts like she has to put up with me and is only helping me because she was ordered to.*

Annie climbed the stairs to her room, locked the door, drew the curtains and crawled into bed. Nestling into the covers, she picked up the forbidden book. The candle on the nightstand provided just enough light to read the ink letters. The pages seemed to fly by and, before she knew it, Annie had already read one-quarter of the book. *I better get to sleep now*, she told herself. Tucking the book safely under her pillow, Annie blew out the candle and closed her eyes.

Down the hall, a shadowy figure stepped slowly up the creaking stairs. It peered under every door crack, looking for light. It listened for the rustling of paper. It looked like a fragment of black wind, but was as dangerous as a sword dripping with poison. The thing was so intent on searching every doorway that it didn't notice when the light in room ten went out.

Annie awoke early in the morning. The sun was still behind the eastern mountains, but the sky was stained purple. She got out of bed quietly and took the book from under the pillow. A hand carved wardrobe stood a few feet from the bed, so she took her box of clothes and placed the book neatly inside the pocket of the vest. She opened the blinds, unlocked the door and went downstairs.

Mr. Beeter was talking to an old lady wearing a white dress. She had silver hair and a tired look on her face. She was holding a wooden spoon in her right hand. *That must be the cook,* thought

Annie. In the far left corner of the room sat five round wooden tables with two chairs under each.

Annie waved at Mr. Beeter, who smiled and motioned for her to come over. He then introduced her to Mrs. Bells, an old friend of his mother. They sat at a table together and ate sausages and sweet cakes. They were careful not to talk about dangerous topics.

"Mrs. Bells, you are a wonderful cook. These cakes are very good," Annie said politely.

Mrs. Bells smiled, said thanks, and took the empty plates into the kitchen. When she left, the innkeeper slipped a note over the table to Annie and put a finger over his lips as if to say, "Don't read it out loud." Annie nodded and unfolded the small paper. It read: *Amy, they are searching frantically for you now. I suggest you leave before anybody else wakes up—for your safety and my family's safety. I have something for you and Mrs. Bells is going to set it on your bed. You best follow her.*

Annie got up, thanked him kindly for the wonderful hospitality he had shown her, and walked off casually. Mrs. Bells passed her in the hall before she reached her room. Checking to make sure nobody was hiding in her closet or under the bed, she locked the door behind her. On the bed sat a large leather bag with a strap she could slip over her shoulder. Peering inside, Annie found five books: *The Eye of Mt. Ablaze, The Siege of Shadows, The Dark Wolf, The Crooked Tree,* and a new one, *Galloping over Air, Water, and Grass.*

The eight-year-old gasped. *These are the forbidden books!*

In addition to the books, Annie found a small red silk bag. Inside were some golden coins engraved with the image of a horse's head. "I can't believe how kind he is," Annie whispered out loud.

A medieval version of beef jerky was packed in a small bundle, along with some ripe fruit that she'd have to eat soon. A loaf of the long-lasting Arfag bread sat next to the other foods.

He somehow knew I was traveling somewhere far. Is there anything in here about me? Annie wondered. A weird feeling filled her stomach and sent it churning. This was getting scarier every minute. Under the bag and the bundle of food lay an old journal with only two pages filled out. It was a letter from Mr. Beeter:

Dear Amy,

I am entrusting you with these books from our past. To have Red as a friend is very dangerous, and she will draw attention that you don't want. I suggest you stay hidden and cover her with oils from the leaves of the tree ivy to hide her scent. I'm also giving you a journal in which to write about your adventures. Hopefully, one day, our children will freely be able to read your story. Don't worry about Mrs. Bell and me. We'll manage. I must warn you, though; "They" are not the only things that hunt in the night. There are also the Toblins and other creatures that surround Mount Ablaze. Stay away from Mount Frost. Toblins swarm over it like ants at work. Beware of plants and animals that seem very interested in you. Give them a false name—as you probably gave me. Mount Frost is littered with crevices and cliffs, not to mention harsh snows and hail. Don't ask me how I know where you are going. There is a prophecy that may involve you. Red is stubborn, but she is a hero. You will read about her past in the books The Siege of Shadows and The Dark Wolf. Know that I'm rooting for you, my dear. When you succeed in your quest, please return to my inn and tell us of your adventures. We'll sit around the table and share drink and sausages.

All my affection and support,
Mr. Beeter

Annie looked down at his note in astonishment. H*ow does he know? How could he know?*

Neatly packing her skirt and pajamas into the bag, Annie slipped on the vest, feeling the book secure in her pocket. She then picked up the bag and walked quietly downstairs. In the stable, she saw Red Mare with her coat brushed and a saddle already on her back. Two saddlebags hung on each side of her shoulders, on her withers.

"How nice!" she exclaimed and ran over to the mare.

"Thank the innkeeper for the saddle. Now let's go."

Again with her negativity, Annie thought. *Why was Red so grumpy? And why is she helping me?*

They trotted out of town, the girl upon her back. Red Mare veered onto a northern trail that led into a thick forest. She started to canter through the shadows and for a few seconds Annie forgot about all her worries. She focused on the wind in her face and the power of the horseflesh under her. After some time, the food in her pack seemed to call to her. It was past noon and the sun beat down mercilessly. She could hear her stomach rumbling. "Red, may I call you Red?"

The horse made some strides in her canter before answering, "Yes."

"Can we stop for lunch? I'm starting to get hungry."

"You humans always think about food!" In truth, the mare's stomach was growling too, and getting the human off her back would be a break.

They stopped near a stream to get a drink. While the mare grazed on the dappled leaves and large apples near the water, Annie sat under a tree with her book and ate some fruit and jerky. They rested comfortably for about an hour, enjoying the sunshine and the sound of birds chattering on the wind. The book was so good that Annie soon finished it. She loved reading fantasy books where anything that normally wouldn't come true, came true. *The Dark Wolf* was next. Annie had a large portion of it finished when Red suddenly trotted over to her and said, "Stop reading. Let's go."

They rode for hours until they came to the edge of the forest. Thick, white clouds hid the mountain from view except for the tiny top peak. It was gleaming white, thousands of feet high.

"Is that Mount Frost?"

"Yes. We might make it in three days' time if we don't stop for anything."

"I don't think I'll be able to do that! I'm so tired."

"Thorn Forest is up ahead. We'll stop there for the night."

"Thorn Forest?"

But Red Mare was already galloping off with her across the field. Worries filled Annie's mind. *Why doesn't she like me? How will I find my sister? Why does the name Thorn Forest frighten me so? What are my parents thinking right now?*

The sky gradually changed to dark orange and pink above the purple mountains. Red galloped onward, hardly breaking a sweat. The dark forest loomed ahead. Vines and bushes filled with thorns hung from the trees, all mingled in a tangled mess. Annie started to feel fearful. The forest looked haunted, as if something long past had been stalking her and now had its chance to jump out at any moment.

The horse stopped on a thin, winding dirt trail. Knowing the danger of camping on a pathway, she picked her way through the bushes and into a small clearing just big enough for the two of them to sleep. The horse stopped with a grumpy snort and the girl hopped off to remove its bridle and saddle. Annie ate a piece of bread and read some more of *The Dark Wolf*. The mare lay down without touching the grass or leaves around her. She appeared to hover above the ground and began to doze as the girl read. Annie was only halfway through the book when the end of a chapter stopped her cold:

> The moon glittered brightly as he lay there, unmoving. Lone One hoped his slate-colored fur would help him blend in with the rocky hills. They were chasing him, and this time they were sure they had trapped him at last. He felt their presence and it sent a shiver up his spine. It was over. Arfag would be destroyed and it would be his fault.

23

"We have you now," a voice hissed behind him.

"Yes, " hissed another. "Your life will now cease, and we will feast!"

Shadowy figures shaped themselves into men. The largest held a silver knife, though the light did not reflect off of the blade. Voices of warning from the prophecies rang in the wolf's sensitive ears. "Beware the knife of the man, a knife poisonous to the mind and does not gleam in the moon."

The knife! I must destroy the knife!

The wolf jumped up and snarled, trying to come up with a plan to take the weapon. A boot knocked him onto his side and held him there, a heavy weight on his neck. Another Thing sneaked up behind him as its leader slowly walked toward the wolf, grinning.

You are no conqueror!" the wolf spat at it. "You'll never win! Arfag will not be destroyed."

The Thing laughed, the sound hollow and cold. It stood over the wolf, grinning. It held up the knife with its claw-like hands and pointed it at Lone One's heart. "You will die now, and then we shall conquer this world, and then earth!"

The wolf's heart pounded. He was about to die!

"Leave!" a thundering voice bellowed like a church bell. The wolf looked up and saw a horse rearing in the moonlight. Three ghost horses were standing behind her.

"She has come!" the wolf howled with joy.

She was the mare, the one the color of the desert sun.

———•———

Red Mare thrashed violently in her sleep. She was standing in a rocky outcrop in the center of the moonlight. A horse flew from the sky like a lightning bolt. It was Sunrise.

"Red Mare!" his voice bellowed. "The girl is being followed. Get out of there now."

"Why? I want nothing to do with the destiny you have made

for me! I want to stay among the Four Hooves and feel freedom. I will not be turned into a mortal horse on earth! I will not!"

"You have chosen to be a member of the Four Hooves," Sunrise reminded her. You are now bound to your destiny!"

Winds as fierce as a hurricane blew around them. "Save the siblings, then face your fate like a noble animal! My filly did. She knew her fate and she knew she would die. She followed her destiny nobly and now she lives with me on the Mountain of Stars."

Red Mare bowed her head, her mane whipping around her neck. "I don't want my fate, yet I want to be part of the Four Hooves!" she yelled. She paused and her voice was quieter now, "Sunrise? Please release me."

"You must accept what the stars have foretold about you. If you refuse, you will become a part of the Eye, which means death. It's your choice, Red Mare. Choose wisely."

"I don't want to die!" she wailed, "I don't want to become part of the Eye. Why must it be I who suffers this fate?"

"You are the one with kindness in your soul. You brought freedom and peace once, and you can do it again. Another horse shall take your place after your quest, and you will live on in the stars."

"Yes, but why *me*?"

"The sacrifice of one preserves the lives of many. You were chosen because you know what it feels like to be beaten and under rule of the evil one."

Understanding began to creep through to her heart, and peace and joy slowly filled her. "So if I give up my hiding place, my shelter, it will provide a haven for others?"

Sunrise nodded, still shining. "Yes, my noble one. You are *joy*! Do not forget that! Because of you, others will not suffer this fate." He reared, but then his ears pinned flat against his head. The scent of blood filled the air.

"Run Red Mare, before they get to you! Wake up! Stop dreaming!" With a worried flick of his tail, he galloped into the sky.

Red Mare couldn't wake: she felt paralyzed. Shadows surrounded her like a vortex, each one whispering an ancient spell.

"No, get out of here! Get away from me!"

The spell completed, they vanished.

Annie woke to see Red sprawled over the grass twitching and gasping for breath. Her eyes were glazed and she was sweating terribly.

"Red! What's wrong?" Fear seized her. "Tell me! Talk to me!"

You must get help," said the mare weakly. "They found me. Hurry!"

"I'll go get help, tell me what to do to save you!"

"The juice of the paraberry. I must have it within one half day. You must get it now!" Again, the mare started twitching and then, suddenly coughing—blood pouring out of her nostrils and her mouth.

Annie slipped the bag over her shoulder and ran back to the trail, into the field. She wanted to scream for help, but she knew it might attract them. What she saw next made her heart feel like it was going to burst: it was the figure of a person riding a black horse. Its hoof beats were silent as it galloped toward her.

Annie ran into the Thorn Forest, blindly running down the trail, her legs aching, her lungs gasping for breath. She could feel the vibrations of the hooves slamming hard on the ground behind her. She could almost feel the animal's breath on her neck when, suddenly, the root of a tree seemed to reach up and trip her. Dirt and pebbles shoved up her nose as her face hit the ground. The rider stopped the horse and both of them stared down on her from above.

"Stay away from me!" Annie wailed.

The rider dismounted and squatted next to her, slowly removing the hood from around its head. It was a girl!

Recognition flooded Annie. She remembered those eyes and gasped: "You're the farm girl from Arfag!"

Chapter 3

The mysterious girl smiled and said, "I knew I'd find you sooner or later."

Annie looked puzzled. "How do you know me?"

The rider laughed, "A little birdie told me." At her words, a tiny robin flew onto her shoulder. It had a white diamond on its chest.

"This is Heart's Song. He's my partner."

"Partner?"

The girl was maybe about thirteen years old. Her long black hair was tied into two braids that hung over her shoulders. Her eyes were emerald green and her skin looked ivory smooth. "This is my horse, Lone One. He was named from a story of a wolf."

Annie heard that name from somewhere—from *The Dark Wolf*, she wondered? "Why did you come for me?"

Her face became serious, and she whispered, "My father is a wizard. In a dream he saw a girl who had a task to fulfill and he knew that she would need help. I offered to go—and so I came."

Annie looked her straight in the eyes and saw no lie. Then, as if by magic, she was suddenly sitting behind the girl on Lone One's back. They galloped out of Thorn Forest as the sky was turning the color of ocean blue.

"What is your name?" Annie asked as they rode over a wide rocky plain.

"My name is Tori. As you guessed, I am a farm girl from the town of Arfag. What is yours?"

"I am Annie. I am from the earth world."

"So, you are far from home. That must be hard."

Heart's Song flew above them at an amazing speed. He chirped as Tori turned Lone One toward the horizon.

A large town rose in the distance. Many buildings stood proudly, some surrounded by farms. None of the buildings were taller than two stories, and they were all made of wood. A marketplace five times bigger than Arfag's lined up and down the streets. Stores were busy, with about a hundred and fifty people crowding the streets. Tori slowed her horse to a trot as they entered the city. The tiny robin landed back on her shoulder, then hid within her hood. Up ahead a sign announced "Framabal Inn, Home of Comfort."

"This place is not as nice as Arfag," Annie muttered.

Her new friend agreed. The people weren't smiling. They all wore fancy clothes and nobody seemed to be talking. Heart's Song chirped quietly in Tori's ear. The girl looked at the edge of the street and saw a creamy brown horse standing hooked to a traveling carriage. A young man stood next to the carriage, reading a book about herbs. The wooden wagon had the word *Medicine* painted on its side in red fancy script. A table near the wagon was crowded with baskets filled with herbs and spices, berries and fruit.

Tori and Annie dismounted and walked over to the young man.

"Good day, ladies!" he called as they approached. "What can I do for you this fine day?"

"We need Paraberries," Annie said. A horse is in urgent need of them before noon. If he doesn't get them, he'll die!"

"Paraberries. I see." He scratched his chin and climbed into the back of his wagon. After a minute or two of rummaging around, he carried out a basket with a label marked *Paraberries: for saving the soul from an evil spell.*

"This is a pretty urgent request. It says here on the label that they must be given within 12 hours of the spell. I don't have them on display because no one has ever asked for them." The young man counted out ten berries and put them carefully in a small cloth bag. "Place five in your horse's mouth; when it wakes, give one more. Every day after, give one more berry until none remain. It should be better after that."

"How much do we pay, sir?" Annie asked politely.

"Oh, no," he laughed, "You don't owe me anything. This is serious and I don't want to profit from your horse's misfortune. I make enough money on other spices and medicine. I'm just glad to be of help"

"Oh, thank you, Sir!" Tori grinned wide in gratitude. "We'll hurry on our way now. Bless your harvest."

"Bless your harvest?" Annie asked as they galloped away.

"In Arfag, we normally say *Bless your harvest*, as a sign of gratitude when someone does something nice for you."

"That is so interesting! I'd like to learn your culture."

Tori laughed as Heart's Song soared over them, singing happily.

"How do you understand him?" Annie asked.

"Down through the ages in Arfag, many of our people kept birds as companions. Often the owners practiced the song language of their birds and gradually they learned to understand and communicate with each other. People then started using birds to spy and gather information when at war. It helped them win many battles over the ages."

The tiny bird swooped up and down singing his joyful song. The sky was getting lighter, and Annie worriedly guessed it was close to noon. Lone One galloped harder, sensing Annie's anxiety, and soon found the trail into Thorn Forest. The tree limbs seemed to reach out to them with thorny vines of fingers, as if trying to stop them from reaching Red Mare in time. The robin flew close to Tori's head and the girls lowered themselves so the branches would not scratch them. Finally, they came to the small side trail that wove into an even smaller clearing. Annie jumped off and ran to her friend. "Red!"

The mare groaned, a puddle of blood soaking the ground. Her brown eyes were covered with misty white goo. *No! Am I too late?* Annie knelt over her horse's noble head and grabbed the berries out of her bag. She fumbled for five of the small red things, slipping each one into Red's mouth. The sun rose higher into the sky—it was a few minutes before noon.

"Oh, Red, don't give up." Tears streamed down Annie's face. She felt guilty about the bad thoughts she had had about her horse. "Don't give in Red! Please!"

The sun hit noon and the mare's eyes rolled back into her head. Her eyelids closed and her breath stopped.

"Red!"

Tori placed a hand on Annie's shoulder, "Maybe now was her time."

"She can't die and leave me here all alone! She was going to help me find my sister!" Tears poured from Annie's eyes as she hugged the mare's bloodstained neck. Heart's Song landed on her shoulder and chirped softly, and Lone One whinnied sadly.

"You must come back to me Red Mare. Please come back!" Annie chanted over and over. "Come back, my friend, my dear friend. Come back to me, Red!"

The horse's neck was now damp with her tears. Tori looked away and sat quietly beside Red Mare's saddle. "Annie, I could help you get to Mt. Frost. You could ride with me on Lone One."

Annie sniffed, "No, Tori. I don't want to endanger your horse. I must do this alone."

"Oh, no, you're not! You know nothing of Toblins or Them. They'd capture you so fast that you wouldn't know what hit you. Remember the knife, Annie? Remember the knife?"

"I don't want you to get hurt," she said again, surprised with her tone of authority. "You'll be safer if you go home and wait for me to return to you."

"No. I'm older and stronger and it is my duty to protect you. I didn't ride all the way out here just to be told to go home. I'm staying with you. You dragged me into this adventure of yours, and now I'm going to help you finish it. Let me go with you to Mt. Frost. I'll distract the Toblins and you'll be able to slip inside their lair and rescue your sister. After that we'll ride back to the nearest city and find another horse. Then, we'll ride back to Arfag together and find my father. He'll help you get back home."

The idea did sound smart. "Alright," said Annie. "Thank you. But please agree that if you, your bird, or your horse are harmed in any way, you will go home immediately."

Reluctantly, Tori agreed.

———

Darkly gray and misty as a shadow, a four-legged figure lurked on the rocky outcrop. There was no moon to show any hint of who the horse was, but a dark vortex twirled around it and a deep voice whispered taunts and jeers.

"Enough! Stop this at once."

The vortex slowed until a large shadow horse stood before the lonely figure.

"Does the fallen pony want comfort?" it teased, as an army of darkness rose from the crags and rocks.

"No, not from you." the figure spat.

"Oh, grumpy are we? Still resisting? Give in pony. Obey the Eye! You will be given power from It, and It will fulfill your purpose. Help us destroy the wolf, the girl, and her friends. Allow us to go back in time and stop your coming, when you save that filthy fleabag. Give in to our power!"

"Never! I will never betray my family."

The army stood silent and ominous.

"Sunrise, I only follow you!"

As they heard the name, the dark army drew back, hissing and growling and snarling.

"The Name! She said the Name!" they whispered evilly.

"I will never stray, Sunrise! Never!"

"Enough of this!" The shadow horse reared and smacked the figure on its head. It fell but got back up proclaiming, "I believe in the Mountain of Stars! In Sunrise's filly! In truth, justice, love and joy! Never will I obey you, Eye, the evil one."

The horse of darkness kicked and bit the figure until she was too weak to say anything else.

"Welcome to the Eye, Red Mare. Welcome to the Eye."

A roar rang in her ears as the army of darkness split to allow a large pathway. A giant mountain lion growled triumphantly and pounced toward the Red Mare and dark horse.

"You shall never see light again and you shall never be rescued," it growled malevolently.

Red Mare looked closer into its eyes; they were filled with fire and hatred.

"The Eye!" she neighed in horror.

"Yes! Come to me with your fear. Feel my hatred!"

A large knife made from silver that did not shine flashed before her. It was almost as big as the mountain lion's head. The blade was bigger than her whole body. "Sunrise! Sunrise!"

Rrrrrrooooaaaaaarrrrrrrr!!!!!!!! His breath was full of malice and his spit was venom.

"Sunrise, save me now!"

"He'll never help you, he can't. He's weak!"

"No!"

The blade turned smaller and smaller, and became the size of an ordinary knife.

"Welcome to the Eye. Give in..." the lion snarled like a dog.

"Nooo!"

The blade came toward her left shoulder, but she kicked it away. It kept coming—again and again, but she resisted.

"Cease this at once!" A voice ringing high, as if from a tower, came from the sky.

"Sunrise!" they all screeched—except for Red Mare, who proclaimed his name as if she were singing to the stars in heaven.

The golden horse landed before the Eye. "Her time has not come, *thing*!" Sunrise declared.

The shadow army cowered before him as he reared and neighed to the sky,

"Be gone evil creatures! You amount to nothing before me! You are like filthy rags!"

The army quivered at his voice and fled into the darkness.

The Eye remained for a moment and snarled, "I will return, Sunrise, and when I do" he spat, turning to Red Mare, "that mare and your world will be mine!" With that, he roared and ran into the darkness.

Chapter 4

Annie walked along the Thorn Forest trail beside Tori, who rode her horse with her bird on her shoulder. They had argued about Annie walking, but the girl had insisted that two saddles, two saddlebags, and a teenager were too much for one horse to carry. Lone One was grateful. Annie trudged along sadly behind with Red Mare's body etched into her mind.

"Annie?"

She didn't answer and kept on walking.

"Annie!"

She refused to talk now, her heart still broken. She blamed herself for Red Mare's death. The last thing on her mind was conversation.

"Annie! You listen to me! I've seen many deaths and I have learned you can't just crawl around, blinded by sorrow. You have to pick yourself up. Red would have wanted you to go on and rescue your sister. Doesn't that mean anything to you?"

"Of course it does! This is so hard. My parents don't seem to care about my sister, and now I've lost Red. What if Louise is lost forever too? What will I do then? I can't just walk home and forget about it! Give me a break!"

"Why did that mare mean so much to you?"

"She had power and joy and wisdom. I sensed it in her. We communicated on a spiritual level. She had a connection with Sunrise and the three white ghost horses."

"Did you say three?"

"Yes, there were four of them in all. There were three ghost horses that opened a portal and chased the Toblins away so that we could get through. They came when Red commanded them."

"Really? Oh my! We need to go back now! She may not be dead!"

"What do you mean? Of course she's dead. I saw her!" Annie wailed. "And it's my fault she died! I couldn't get the berries to her fast enough! I fumbled with them and fed them to her too close to noon. I forgot to make her swallow them! They are probable still in her mouth right now!" She slumped down onto the trail, tears streaming down her face.

Tori sighed, "Come on, you couldn't help it. I should've let you ride Lone One and we would have gotten there sooner. But I didn't and we got there right at noon. It's not all your fault, but listen! There may be hope that she's not really dead. Let's hurry!"

Tori leaned down with an outstretched hand, "Come on now, onto your feet!"

Reluctantly, Annie grabbed her hand and jumped onto Lone One's back and wrapped her arms around Tori's waist. The small group cantered back to the mare's death spot.

Tori jumped off and ran into the small clearing, "Annie! Annie, come here!"

Annie slowly dismounted and led the horse into the clearing where the dead body lay covered in light. Suddenly, the body disappeared! They stood staring at the indented spot where the mare had been, feeling frightened.

"Look over there, Annie! The field! The field!"

They ran to the distant field where the blue sky was dark and cloudy. A black spot appeared in the center of the storm clouds.

Are they coming? Annie wondered.

A slash of lightning split through the black spot and, as it did, a red shape galloped out, coming down like a peregrine falcon on its dive. The figure landed a few yards away from them, her mane and tail flowing in the breeze; her head tall and proud.

"Red!"

The mare reared and whinnied happily as the girl ran toward her.

Annie wrapped her hands around Red's soft neck feeling joyful and grateful. Red stood calmly as Annie climbed onto her back.

"I'm glad you're back," she whispered.

"I'm glad too." Let's go find your sister!"

Tori mounted her steed and followed them on the path to the deadly forest. All were glad to run with the sun on their faces. Heart's Song flew above them singing cheerfully.

"What happened to you after I fed you the berries?"

"That is something you'll never want to know. Trust me on this." Red said.

"It was that horrible?"

"Yes, but I'll tell you this much. *They* tried to get me to join them and I wouldn't be here with you riding on my back if they had. You would be dead and I would be in eternal blackness."

"Annie," Tori interrupted, "Will you take your saddle back now? Lone One is tiring of it."

"Of course."

Tori stopped her black horse and Annie grabbed the saddle and placed it on Red Mare.

Framabal Town stood proudly in the distance but the group didn't bother to stop. The sun was high and the road was flat and they were making good time, so they galloped past the wooden sign that read, 'Come Visit Framabal Town: A Place of Your Desire.'

It was almost sunset, but the journey continued for miles. They decided to stop and sleep under the stars and leave refreshed, first thing in the morning.

Tori bit her lip. "I don't think this is a good idea. We can be seen for miles from any direction. If we are sleeping, we won't see anyone sneak up on us."

"I can sense a dark presence even when I sleep," Red reassured her. "You don't have anything to worry about."

They all lay down in the soft grass. It was too dark to see the ink words so Annie went to sleep without reading her book. Tori watched as Annie curled up in the curve of the mare's neck.

Humph, she thought, *Annie really loves her. I wonder what her life was like on the earth world?*

Lone One was already asleep with Heart's Song on her shoulder. *They look so peaceful together*, Tori thought with a smile. Not feeling sleepy, she looked up at the sky and noticed the moon was thinning. She sensed something was agitating the red mare, as the horse was restless and snorting in her sleep. All was silent as Tori walked away from the camp, and after going a short way, she sat down and closed her eyes. A voice suddenly spoke in her head,

"Tori? Can you hear me?"

"Yes, Father, I can."

"How are you, dear?"

"I'm well, but I'm worried our enemies are close at hand. Can you sense them, too?"

"Yes, yes, I can. I would get out of there soon if I were you. Have you found the girl?"

"Yes. She is sleeping with the horses and all are hidden in the high grass. They'll be angry if I wake them."

"If you don't wake them now they'll be killed! If they don't listen, ride away anyway. I don't want you getting hurt."

"No, father, I won't be disloyal to my friends."

"Very well. Warn them. I'll be searching for you. Tomorrow night?"

"Yes, we'll talk again tomorrow night."

Tori stood up feeling a little light headed. *Having a wizard for a father had its advantages! I won't get much sleep tonight*, she thought. She ran as quietly as a mouse back to camp. "Wake up, wake up!" She shook Annie until she opened her eyes. Red stirred and Lone One grunted.

"What is it Tori?"

"I sense them. They are near."

"I smell them," Red whispered.

Lone One reared in fright and the robin chirped in terror.

"Quickly! Get the saddles on us!" Red ordered.

Annie and Tori frantically tacked up their horses. Just as the water recedes before a tsunami, the air did the same thing. It receded so fast they couldn't breathe—and then it rushed back with a mighty force that knocked more air out of them. Black shapes of men riding horses galloped toward them. Some transformed into birds and flew through the air with a deadly beauty.

"Heart's Song, stay with me!" Tori yelled as she mounted.

The little robin hopped into the hood hanging down Tori's back. Annie hopped onto a rock and jumped onto Red Mare's back, her heart beating like a war drum as they galloped off. Shadow falcons flew above them and dark horses with riders waved swords behind them.

"Why do they change?" Annie asked as they glided over a rock.

"To intimidate you! They're getting closer!" Tori yelled behind them.

A falcon was dove at Annie's head and a phantom rider swung a sword inches from Lone One's back legs. Red Mare reared and galloped back, whispering prayers as she went.

In a sudden burst of light, Annie saw that a glowing sword appeared in her hand. It gleamed like diamonds. She raised it high and hit the falcon with its sharp point. It screeched and vanished into black smoke.

The red mare reared again and came down on the black horse and its rider. They lay sprawled out on the ground, stunned. As the mare turned away, ten more Things tripped over the fallen figures, causing more to fall.

"Road block!" Red jeered and they raced off toward a small town that loomed in the distance. It gleamed with a blue glow.

Red swung her head from side to side and lengthened her stride. When they reached the town they slowed to a walk so the sound of hooves would not wake the residents. In the dim light of the moon they saw a harbor full of ships. Many had tall masts and wooden carvings of dragons, ladies, fairies, or birds on the front.

"Wow," Annie whispered as they passed through the streets. A large sea stretched out before them, and, despite the time of night, sailors and townsfolk filled the docks and ships. The dark army vanished. Inns and shops filled the streets. Houses were two stories high and built right next to each other, some sharing a common wall.

"They ruin perfectly good houses putting them so close together." Tori mumbled. "Where's the yard and farms? Its terrible not to have privacy!" The others ignored her ranting. At the edge of the main road, a small dirt path angled off through some trees. "Let's go through there. It might lead us to some decent farms," she suggested.

"Let's make Tori happy, Red."

Red Mare nodded and they started down the trail. After passing through a small thicket, they came upon a house with a stable.

"Now, here are some smart people!" Tori smiled.

"See, we made her happy," Annie whispered.

The stable was small, with three stalls and three horses. The horses lifted their heads and pawed the ground when they heard the travelers' approach. The visitors sneaked around to the back of the stable and found a place to rest out of view. The sky was getting lighter as they fell asleep, not knowing the people in the house were waking.

⸺•⸺

Annie opened her eyes as light streamed into them. She blinked and saw a frowning boy standing over her. In his hand he held the reins of a white horse.

"Who are you?" he asked in a nervous voice.

After her eyes got used to the light, the girl replied, "We were traveling and chased into this town by some bandits. We needed a place to sleep and were hoping not to bother you. We mean no harm." She didn't want to scare him about the shadow figures.

Annie looked to her right and saw Tori still sleeping, her head resting on her saddle. Lone One was nowhere to be seen. Then Annie realized that Red Mare was nowhere to be seen either.

"Red! Lone One! What did you do to them?" she demanded.

Her loud outburst woke Tori. "What's wrong?" she mumbled.

"My parents led them away," the boy stammered. "They don't appreciate trespassers. They're taking them to the auction down in Framabal Town, which starts at noon. They plan on sending the sheriff after you when they get there."

"What?" the teen cried in disbelief, "You stole our horses?"

Framabal Town? Again? Annie's legs felt like ten pounds of stone. *Did they really have to go all the way back*?

"You listen here, boy," Tori screamed, trying to keep from strangling him in her fright and anger. "You had no right to take them. We want them back. Now!"

"Sorry, you'll have to talk to my parents about it. I'm not allowed to help you."

"You little…"

"Tori, stay calm. We'll get them back." Annie looked at the boy and asked in a kinder voice, "What is your name, young man?"

"Um...my name is Grack."

"Grack, we really need our horses back. They are both dreadfully ill and need to be taken to a veterinarian. That's why we slept out here and not in the stable. We didn't want the sickness to spread to your horses. We need to get help for them soon!"

His smug expression turned into a look of worry. "My horse might sick?"

"I don't think so, but you can never be sure. We must hurry. You don't want to have all of those horses at the auction to get the awful disease, do you?"

"No!"

"Good. Now ride with us and help us get our horses back."

"I'm not so sure. My parents…"

"Ride with us on your fastest horse. If we try and get away, you may turn us in to the sheriff."

He nodded solemnly, glancing at Tori as she shook the dirt off her skirt. Annie realized that Tori probably looked intimidating to someone who didn't know her. She wore a black cape and walked around with a bird on her shoulder. She had a temper too, but Annie was glad she was her friend.

Grack told them to stay where they were while he ran into the stable to get the other horses.

Tori whispered, "Nice lie, very convincing."

"Thanks."

"All right, you two can come in and tack up with your own saddles!" Grack called from inside the barn.

Hoisting their tack into their arms, the girls walked into the shade of the stable. It had a dirt floor and three wooden stalls, each having a name carved into it. A couple of horses stood outside the stalls tied to two posts. One horse was a tall, mouse grullo; the other was small and chocolate brown; barely thirteen hands. Annie assumed she would get the short horse, but Grack stopped her.

"No, you get the mare," he ordered.

The mare was taller than Red! Her saddle was too thin for this horse and the girth strap wasn't long enough.

They all mounted and when Annie looked over at Tori, she almost burst out laughing. The tall teen was given the shorter horse and her legs almost touched the ground. Tori look annoyed as they rode out of the barn.

"Why did you put me on this tiny horse?" Tori whined.

Grack laughed until he couldn't breathe. "So you won't get any ideas of escaping! He's my slowest horse!"

Tori emitted a small growl.

Annie's horse was far too big for her, and she knew it would be hard for her to escape too. *But I don't want to escape! I want Red back.*

It was almost noon as they cantered to town, Tori galloped just to keep up.

A thought came to Annie. *If we catch up and tell them about the horse sickness, will they give us our horses back or will they demand proof? Maybe Red will help. She knows what I am thinking.*

They saw two shapes on horseback walking in the distance. By the flicking red tail of one of the horses, Annie knew it was Red Mare. Grack moved ahead and Annie slowed down to ride next to her friend.

"Tori, I have an idea. Grack's parents are going to want proof of this sickness. Send Heart's Song to tell our horses to start coughing and walk lamely."

Tori nodded and whispered to the robin. He chirped and flew off like a lightning bolt. After the bird's return, they could see their horses stumbling and heard fake coughs in the distance. Because the stumbling slowed the horses down, Grack and the girls caught up with them soon. As they neared, Annie heard a gruff voice swearing at Red for her sudden "bad" behavior. A gruff man smacked the mare and told her to move onward.

"Stop hitting her! Annie cried. "She's sick!"

The man and woman stopped and turned to look.

"Who do you think you are, telling me what to do with my horse?" Grack's father demanded.

"She's not yours. She's mine. You stole those horses from us!" Annie protested.

"Grack, what are you doing here with those two?" the woman asked. "We told you to wait for the sheriff!"

"I'm sorry, Mom, but their horses have a disease, and it can spread to the other horses at the auction!"

"How do you know that's the truth?" his father asked, looking at the girls with suspicious eyes.

Annie dismounted and pulled out the small brown bag. She took out the Paraberries and walked over to the mare, who was now adding a nice touch of drool.

"Hi, girl," Annie soothed and ran her hand over the noble face.

Red whinnied and her fake coughs filled the air.

"Here, have some medicine."

She placed a paraberry into Red's mouth and watched as she swallowed it. Grack's father watched closely as well.

"What about the other one?" he asked.

Drool was dripping out of Lone One's mouth too. *She must be copying Red! Annie thought.* She fed a berry to Lone One too and looked at the parents with innocent eyes. "Please. Give us our horses back."

"Why were you on our land last night? We saw you sneaking behind the stable. Were you planning to steal our horses?"

"I'm sorry about that. We were chased into town by bandits and followed the dirt trail that led to your house. We didn't want to wake you, so we hid behind the stable. We also didn't want your horses to get sick."

Grack's father was very suspicious and took his time studying their faces. He sensed they were lying, but he didn't want to take a chance and sell sick horses. It would ruin his reputation.

Grack's mother hadn't wanted to sell the horses in the first place. She just wanted to give the girls a warning and send them off. Bandits wouldn't sleep behind a stable. They'd be gone with their horses in a matter of minutes. She dismounted and said, "Here, take your horses. A bandit would have stolen our animals, not slept behind the stable."

Tori dismounted, un-tacked her saddle, and placed it on Lone

One faster than a bullet leaving a gun. She hugged her horse around the neck and offered soothing words. She wiped the drool off the horse's lips and patted her neck.

Red snorted and gave a false cough. The boy's father dismounted and walked over to his wife. Annie un-tacked the tall mare and placed her own bridle and saddle on Red Mare. She handed Grack's saddle and bridle to the father.

"Thank you, kind sir," she said politely. "You made the right decision."

"Go before we change our minds," he growled.

The two mounted and galloped off toward the harbor town again.

Chapter 5

It was evening by the time they reached the harbor town. Annie was so tired she wondered how she managed to gallop all the way back to the harbor without falling off. Tori looked exhausted, too.

"Red, how come you didn't call me when you were stolen?"

"I didn't want to scare the humans. They probably never heard a normal horse talk before."

"Well, you could've shown them who you really are. They had horses; they're probably good people."

The noble horse shook her desert red mane, "Never judge a person because they own a horse. They could be as rotten as a grave."

Annie yawned sleepily and tried to sit up straight, "Where do we go next?"

"We must cross the sea. We'll need to get onto one of those ships."

Tori's thoughts snapped back from a daydream. "A ship? We're going on a ship? No, No! No! No!"

Lone One flattened her ears and backed up nervously, sensing her rider's distress.

"What's so bad about ships, Tori?" Annie asked.

"I had a brother who moved here to work on the boats. He worked on a ship called the Sea Unicorn. It had a narwhal on the bow. One night my father saw in a dream that my brother was unloading a box off the ship when something overcame him. It took him away—and four other crewmembers as well. The next day, the captain found one of my brother's shoes washed up on the shore. They never found any sign of the crew. That was a year ago—on the other side of *that* sea. My father never had any more visions about what happened."

"I'm so sorry." Annie said. "Would you rather stay here? We'll go on ahead and come back to get you after we find my sister." Annie didn't pay attention to the mare shifting uncomfortably under her.

"I'm not sure," Tori said. "I don't want to be disloyal to you. I'll think about it."

"You'd better decide quickly because we're leaving this evening," the mare said waving her tail.

A breeze started to churn the blue water. The horse's hooves made a clicked-clack sound as they walked along the harbor. The wooden pathways stretched far into the water so that people could get onto the ships without getting wet. The harbor was packed with people carrying bags and animals; others were swabbing the decks or selling items. Tori looked at the churning water and started to feel seasick. She imagined it turning red with blood, the blood of her brother and crewmates. She decided right then not to go. Tori turned Lone One around quickly, and as soon as they reached the street, they galloped away.

"Tori!"

"Leave her be, Annie, said Red. "She's terrified of water."

"I'll miss her. Do you think she'll be here waiting for us when we come back?"

Once again Annie missed the mare's uneasy shift beneath her body. "I'm sure she will," Red said without conviction.

"Which ship are we going on?" Annie asked.

"The Sea Unicorn."

"*What?* The Sea Unicorn? That's Tori's brother's boat!"

"Yes, and its probably just as well that she decided not to go."

"Can't we go onto a different ship?" A feeling of dread crept up her spine.

"Unless you want to have an extra week of riding, going on that boat is the fastest way to Mount Frost."

Annie's legs felt like ten pounds of stone at the thought of riding for an extra week. "Okay, let's go on the Sea Unicorn."

After many minutes of shuffling their way through the crowd, Red and Annie finally arrived at the largest boat in the harbor. It had a wooden carving of a narwhal pointing its horn forward on the bow. Hardly any crewmen or passengers walked along the boat or deck. A short, chubby man stood next to the plank and looked up from his daydream as they approached.

"So, ye want to ride the Sea Unicorn, do ye?"

"Yes sir, how much will it be?" Annie asked as politely as she could.

"Not much Miss, not since 'The Incident.'"

"How much is it?"

"Them crewmen were quite the happy ones they were. Always going about their business, not a bother to nobody, they were."

"How much will it cost, sir?"

"I miss them fellows, I sure do. One was my nephew, you see; he was a cheery lad, he was."

"How *much is it,* sir?" Annie was losing her patience.

"Oh, I already told ye! Missies like you never listen! Two coins Miss, two coins."

Annie pulled out two coins from her bag. The horse heads upon them gleamed in the setting sun as she dropped them into his hand. Looking at them and back up at her he said, "You're an Arfag lass, ain't you? Nice place there. Nice place."

With a nod, Annie dismounted, and led the mare up the steep plank to the deck. A tall man stood in the middle of the ship, looking off into the distance. When he saw them he smiled and walked over. "Hello Miss, I'm the captain of this ship. Welcome aboard."

Annie liked this person much better than the man who collected the coins. He had a straightforward manner and made a nice impression.

"Thank-you. I need a place for my horse and me. Do you have any room?"

His cheerful face became solemn. "Ever since 'The Incident,' there has always been enough room."

"She's from Arfag, Cap'n." The coin collector ran up the plank holding the two gold coins high in the air. "I've got proof with these here coins!" The chubby man seemed ecstatic.

The captain laughed, "Well, now Miss, would you like a room with a stall next to it?"

"Yes, please. That would be perfect."

"Follow me, and watch your step. This ramp is slippery."

They went through a doorway that led down into the passenger area. There were round windows all along a long hall. He stopped at room five that was next to a stall.

"I can't say that this is a fancy room, but it should be adequate for three days. Enjoy the voyage." With that said, he tipped his hat and walked off.

Annie opened the stall door and led the mare in. It was small and musty and had old hay on the floor. There was a little rack to hang her saddle, saddlebags, and bridle. Feeling tired, Annie slumped down onto the hay and fell asleep, cuddled up to her horse's back. She forgot there was a room next door.

Annie woke in the early morning feeling stiff, sore, and hungry. She reached into her saddlebag and pulled out a piece of stale bread. Feeling thirsty, she got up and quietly went into the hall looking for water. The light of dawn crept through the round windows. She was about to go up the ramp when she heard a soft girlish cry. Someone was sitting in the shadows against the wall. She walked over and softly said, "Hello?"

The small girl's face was red and wet; she was around five years old. Sniffling, she turned away.

"Why are you crying?" Annie inquired. *This girl reminds me so much of my sister.* "Can I help you in some way?"

"I... I don't know. I'm bored and lost and lonely!"

Annie sat down beside her and the little girl looked away.

"Do you like horses?"

In an instant the girl looked up and nodded. Annie smiled, knowing she had hit on the right topic.

"I have a horse as red as the desert sun. Would you like to see her?"

At once the girl dried her tears and smiled happily. "Oh, yes, please!"

Annie led her to the stall and opened the door. Red Mare was already up and sniffing around the place. When she saw her partner enter with the little girl, she neighed softly and rubbed her nose against the girl's cheek in a greeting.

"See, she likes you."

The small girl laughed and hugged the horse. "Your horse is red!" she exclaimed.

Annie sat down in the hay, "What is your name?" she asked.

"My name is Sarbra."

Sarbra had blond hair with blue eyes that sparkled. With a happy laugh, she sat down next to Annie.

"Where is your room?"

"I don't know. I went for a walk and I couldn't find my way back." The boat creaked and the wind moaned along the hallway.

"I'm going up on deck. Want to join me? We can look for your room together."

"Yes, please," she said, softly kissing the mare's soft nose as they left.

When they reached the deck, it was wet with rain. They noticed that the captain had set a small table under the overhang of his cabin. He sat on a stool peeling something round and purple. The table held a large bowl of bread and fruit, and large bucket nearby was full of fresh water.

Fruit? Doesn't fruit rot? Annie was perplexed.

The captain got up from his seat and called over to them, "Come on you two! No use being hungry and wet. Come eat something." He smiled at them and Annie noticed that one of his front teeth was missing.

Huddling under the overhang, the girls ate fruit and bread.

"Why do you have fruit on board, doesn't it rot?" asked Annie.

"We only serve it on the first day of the journey. We get fresh fruit every time we dock." He flashed another toothless smile.

The fruit looked odd, and Annie knew that on earth this kind of fruit didn't exist. Sarbra ate the last of her bread and grabbed a ladle full of water, drinking half of it in one gulp. Annie eagerly drank too. *It's going to be a long three days*, she thought.

The Sea Unicorn had been gone for two days, but the dock was still filled with people milling around. Guilt clung to her like a leech as Tori sat upon her horse and searched the horizon for the long departed vessel. She looked haughty and proud on the outside, but she was miserable on the inside. She spent most of her time walking through the woods near the hills around the sea.

It was a rainy day again as she walked along an old overgrown pathway. She heard a voice through the trees and stopped to listen. Not many creatures that lived in these woods talked.

"Now, is our chance, just like last year. We will raid the boat and capture the two who pose a threat to us," a shadowy voice said in anticipation.

"I'm not sure. They're smart and strong and they have allies all around. It's risky and dangerous," another said.

"Stop it," said a third, sounding more sinister than the rest. "We'll drag the girl up to Mount Frost on the night of no moon. Toblins will swarm around her and soon nothing will be left. Then we'll take the horse into the Shadow Realm as a sacrifice offering. Nothing will be left of her after the Eye is done with her."

"What about that teen with the wizard father? She's around somewhere. What do we do if we find her?" the second one asked.

Tori felt a catch in her breath and her heart skipped a beat as the third one snickered, "We'll take her apart piece by piece … by the way, little missy, we know you're there."

Tori screamed and galloped out of the forest and into the town. Although she rode as fast as she could, the creatures followed, nipping at Lone One's heels. Tori directed Lone One to keep running until they were out of the town. The creatures disappeared as they ran along the forest ridge that dropped into the churning sea. *I must warn my friends,* she thought.

———

Annie sat in the stall reading the last pages of *The Dark Wolf*. After the chilling ending, she grabbed the next book: *The Siege of Shadows*. The cover was worn from use.

"That one might give you some important information about the shadow army," Red Mare mentioned as the girl picked it up. "It might help us in some way."

Hours went by silently, except for an occasional horsy snort, or the turning of a page. It was the evening of the second day. Sarbra was returned to her parents yesterday, and Annie hadn't seen her since. The books were her only past time now, except for the occasional talk with Red. Annie wasn't sure why, but the horse wanted to keep her talking ability a secret. At night, Annie's dreams were filled with running and shadows, (?)screaming and fighting. Red seemed to have fitful dreams as well. The ship held a mystery and had an effect on them. It was late when Annie blew out her candle and closed her eyes.

> She dreamed she was walking down a forest path and heard voices. Something made her scream, but she didn't know what. She ran and ran, but never seemed to get anywhere. Suddenly she was sitting in deep snow; the wind blew in her eyes and her bottom felt frozen. Her hands were blue and slithering shapes were all around her. Something screamed inside her again and then—everything went dark. When she opened her eyes she could hear footsteps and hoof-beats; she could smell the coppery

scent of blood. Screams and screeches split the sky. She looked up and saw millions of stars, but it was a night of no moon.

Red Mare dreamed she walked along a path of stone. Cave walls surrounded her and shapes shifted around her. She didn't know how she happened to be in this cave. She passed by two statues, one to her left and another to her right. They were gruesome figures of vampires with wings and real blood dripping down the fangs. They were illuminated by an eerie green light. She tried to stop; every instinct told her to, but something wouldn't let her. She entered a chamber with many more horrific statues and gargoyles. A throne covered in spider webs rose before her in the center of the room. Statues of mountain lions surrounded it, as well as a pool of bubbling, glowing acid. Shadow shapes slithered all around, giving off mournful, evil moans. A large shape appeared on the throne and laughed a laugh that shook the soil above. Red couldn't see the sky, but she knew that above her was a night of no moon.

They both woke up sweating and panting. Annie snuggled next to the mare and tried to get back to sleep, but sleep never returned.

It was getting hot on the ship and the hay stuck to them. They were glad when it was morning as Annie led Red upstairs to get some fresh air. It was raining still, but they welcomed it. It cooled their burning faces and beating hearts.

"Red?"

"What is it?"

"Did your dream involve a night with no moon?"

The mare stopped breathing for a second, "Yes."

"Was there screaming and frozen mountains and darkness?"

"There was darkness alright, and yes, it was cold."

"Was it a dream or a vision of the future?"

"I don't know. Let's hope they were just nightmares."

The captain had his food table set up again, and Annie grabbed a couple ladles of water. She drank a full one and half of a second, pouring the rest onto the mare's dry lips. Red licked it gratefully. The water felt good on their parched throats, so they drank more. They stood in the rain for a while longer and enjoyed the mist on their faces.

Her horse was breathing heavily, but Tori rode him at the fastest gallop ever. Her bird rode on her shoulder and gazed silently ahead. He hadn't sung or chirped in days, and Tori was worried. *What if he is sick?* The rain beat down like thunder onto the ground and she wasn't sure if she was ahead of the shadow creatures or behind them. Fear kept her galloping through the trees. The third day was almost over. *What would happen if she didn't get there in time?* Fearing the worst, and her horse slick with sweat, Tori tried to make up time and meet the boat at the dock.

"Everybody, pack your bags, we are docking in one hour!" The captain went into the passenger area knocking loudly on the doors. Annie stood and hoisted the brown saddle onto the mare's back. She slipped the saddlebags on next. Then she slipped on her vest, placing her book in the pocket. She carefully led her horse up the ramp and onto the deck area. People were already crowding together, leaning on the railings and looking out at the land. Sarbra waved goodbye to them timidly, holding her mother's hand.

Red sniffed the air, "They're here, Annie. They are waiting for us."

"Oh, no, are you sure?" The thought of the shadow creatures scared Annie and made her stomach twist. What they had done to Red Mare—wouldn't they do the same to her?

The girl and horse sat listening to people chatter about how glad they were to see land. Annie wanted to stay on the ship where it felt safe, even though she knew it was an illusion.

An hour passed and they began to dock. Crewmen set up the planks and the passengers started to file down with Red and Annie following. The area around the harbor was small, with several shops selling fruit, water, bread, ropes and supplies. Derelict lifeboats sat rotting next to the dock. There were no roads or walkways, just a small mossy clearing surrounded by a forest.

"*They're* near," Red whinnied.

Annie mounted and the two began a nervous trot toward an old forest path.

An invisible voice hissed, "We found you." Suddenly, twenty shadowy figures emerged like clouds through the trees. People nearby screamed and ran back onto ships or down the sandy bank. The figures surrounded Annie and Red, shifting into many different forms.

"Leave us alone! You don't scare us!" Annie screamed and kicked at a thing when it got too close.

"Brave words for a child so small. Look into my eyes and let's see how brave you really are," it hissed.

"Don't listen! Close your eyes!" Red shouted, but it was too late.

Annie looked into fiery red, yellow, and green eyes. Within them she saw the reflection of a person, a girl. It looked like Louise, and she was crying. Annie wanted to reach out and comfort her but the shapes came between them and started to cluster all around Louise. They lunged forward and tore her apart. Blood was spouting everywhere. Annie screamed and watched with horror as the reflection in the creature's eyes showed the same thing happening to her. The vision changed again, showing Red Mare being thrown into the glowing pool of green acid. A dark shape laughed as Annie watched her beloved horse dissolved alive.

She tried to look away from the awful pictures but couldn't, and screamed as the scent of blood and death wrapped around her.

Annie was oblivious to Red's voice calling out to break the spell. Cold wet hands gripped her arms and she screamed again as they tried to drag her away. She felt paralyzed.

"Annie, wake up! It's a dream, just a nightmare, wake up!"

Nothing mattered to her now. Fear and hopelessness engulfed her. The shadows absorbed the dim light and she could hardly see the mare rearing and fighting. Then an image came to her from on high. It was a golden horse shining with the glorious light of dawn. His mane and tail waved colors in the wind. The scent of blood faded away, replaced by pine-scented meadows and dew- covered flowers. A cool breeze blew on Annie's face. The magnificent stallion cantered gracefully and powerfully toward her. His noble head and neck were slightly bent, like an Arabian.

"Annie, Annie...."

She looked up at him, but couldn't speak. She felt the shadows loosen their grip.

"Awaken, Annie! Awaken!" his voice boomed like a church bell and rang in her head (?). He reared and she focused her eyes.

"Annie, Annie!" Red reared too, trying to get loose, calling her name.

The black glaze melted from her eyes; the pictures were gone and she could think again. She became filled with rage.

"Your filthy images could not hold me!" she screamed at the army of darkness.

"Sunrise!" Red Mare neighed to the heavens, "Sunrise! You've come!"

The creatures wilted back a little more, and the girl broke free. Sunrise whispered an ancient spell "arabracus momentum..." and soon a glowing, white sword was in Annie's hand. She charged at the fifteen figures holding Red. Holding the sword over her head, she screamed, "Leave my horse alone!" She cut the rope and knocked ten shadows down with a few swipes of her blade. The mare kicked loose.

Tori could see the commotion in the distance and pressed forward, wiping the salty sweat from her eyes. Reaching the dock she screamed "Yaaaaaa!" and raced into the battle with a silver sword in her hands, her cape flowing behind her. She galloped over some of the creatures and knocked down five more. The creatures were taken off guard and never had time to shift into something else.

Annie made her way to the largest cloud of blackness swarming around the Eye. She raised her sword and cried, "You will never defeat us!"

It bellowed in contempt and swirled into the air higher and higher until its spread wings had morphed into a fifty-foot dragon. Its cold eyes glared at her as it tried to shred the girl with its open claws. Opaque, black fire flamed out of its mouth and made her step back. The stench was nauseating. Annie could smell the ash and fire as it licked at her hair and clothes, even in the wet darkness. She held the sword higher and it glowed brightly, like the full moon. "This is for Tori's brother!" she cried, as ran it into the stomach of the creature.

"Nooooo!" it screeched.

The light from the sword flowed through the creature, turning it into a black cloud that grew smaller and smaller until it disappeared.

In its place stood five crewmen.

Chapter 6

"Brother!"

Tori dismounted and ran to a young man who had similar brown hair and eyes. The men were surrounded by light and looked around bewildered, as if waking up from a long sleep.

"No, Tori!" Red Mare warned as she blocked her from running to them.

"Why?" Tori asked, looking up at the horse with anger and confusion, "He's my brother! I haven't seen him in a year! Get out of my way!"

"Tori! It's good to see you, her brother said. Why won't that horse let you come to me?"

"Don't listen to him, he's trying to trick you!" Red Mare waved her mane around her noble face. "Don't!"

"I thought you were my friend. Now you won't let me see my own brother?"

"Some things are not as they seem, Tori," Red warned again.

"You think you can trust someone; then they betray you," the brother shouted. "Come to me, Tori. Come to me, Sis. I've missed you so much!"

Tori tried to swerve around the mare, but Red remained impassable.

"Let me through!" Pushing the horse aside, Tori yelled for Heart's Song. "Heart's Song, land on my brother's shoulder and show Red there is nothing to be afraid of."

The robin refused to move and chirped angrily as it shook its little head no.

"Come to me, Tori, hurry! If I don't touch human hands, I will turn to dust! Please, I don't have much time left."

"Red! Let me through!" She was furious now, feeling out of control. She unsheathed her sword, "Move or else."

"Tori! Now, please!"

"I'm coming, brother,"

"I hate to do this, but you leave me no choice!" The mare reared and knocked the sword out of Tori's hands. It dropped to the ground with a clank. Tori made a dash for her brother and, before the mare could stop her, her hands clasped his.

"Nooooo!" Red Mare tried to kick them apart but it did no good.

All watched in horror as Tori's eyes started to glaze over, the light turning grey around them. The crewmen started to change; turning into creatures so horrifying that Annie needed to shield her eyes.

"Annie! Save me, Annie," Tori yelled, looking back at her, her eyes continuing to glaze.

"Don't listen to anything they say, Tori. Block your ears if you have to. They want you to become one of them."

Annie ran at them with her sword. "I destroyed you once, and I will again. Wake, Tori! Wake!"

But Tori's eyes changed into those of a predator and she began to charge. In defense, Annie plunged her sword into the darkening heart. As soon as it entered the flesh, a terrible guilt washed over her. *What am I doing stabbing my friend? Or am I killing a creature?*

Those black eyes looked straight into hers, blank and impassive. "Annie, what are you doing?" the creature Tori whispered in a choking, fading voice.

Annie kept the sword in place and Tori dropped to the mossy ground. The brother and crewmen formed into shadow clouds and scattered through the trees.

"Did I kill her?" Annie finally had enough nerve to ask the question out loud. She pulled the sword out but there was no blood on the blade.

The mare looked at her with her deep, brown eyes.

"No. She's knocked out and recovering. You saved her. If you have anymore of those paraberries, you should give one to her and also eat one yourself. It will hold them off for a while and will make you stronger and better able to ward off future attacks."

Annie sat down and looked through the saddlebags, her hands shaking. She took out two berries, popped one in her mouth, and went over to Tori and placed one into her mouth as well. The veil over Tori's eyes slowly started to lift.

"I don't understand. What happened back there after I stabbed the dragon?" Annie asked.

Red answered, "It didn't die. It can't die. It just thought of another way to fool you and test your wits. You could have been killed trying to save your friend when one of them pretended to be her brother. I've learned never to believe what they want you to believe. You *must* watch your path and where your mind goes. Never forget to watch your back—and always have your sword at the ready."

Red's words blended into the lavender scented night. It was as if the glowing stallion was still there watching her. She could almost hear him whisper in her head, "*Annie, Awaken! Awaken! Be aware of your surroundings!*"

Her eyes opened and she saw Red staring at her. "Red! I had the strangest dream! Do you know anything about a glowing stallion with a voice like a church bell?"

"Did he glow with the light of dawn?"

Annie nodded and Red smiled. "That's Sunrise. He's the Ruler of this world. Not many get to see him, so, you are very fortunate. Most people here don't believe in him, but all of the animals do."

Tori began to stir and sat up holding her head. "What was *that* all about? What happened to me? Why does my chest hurt?"

Annie expected the mare to pour criticism all over Tori for disobeying, but instead she turned to her and frowned. "You were tricked and almost became one of them."

Heart's Song chirped happily and hopped onto her shoulder singing his favorite song. Lone One, who for the most part had been huddling in the shade of the trees, ran to Tori and nuzzled her. Tori, however, seemed to just notice the bitter berry in her mouth. She swallowed it, though with a wave of coughing afterward. "What was that?"

"A paraberry, to help you regain your strength. Annie saved your life," Red replied.

Tori's face was blank for a moment. Slowly, she turned to her friend. "You did?"

"You just went through a terrible ordeal", Annie said. "You were tricked in the most hurtful way with the memory of your brother shoved in your face. You should get some rest; I think you'll need it." Annie turned her back to her and walked off, trying to keep from crying.

"What's wrong with her?" the teen asked the red mare.

"She's been traumatized, too," the mare replied. "She had to stab her friend in the heart!"

"What do you mean she stabbed me in the heart?"

Red snorted in annoyance. *Why did the girl have to ask this question over and over?"*

"She had to—in order to save your life! Like it or not, she did it and you are still here, living and breathing. You should be grateful!"

"I still don't get it, though," Tori persisted. "How could she do that even though it might have killed me?"

"You would have died peacefully or lived forever in the shadow.

Either way would have been death. You're lucky living was an option!" Red retorted.

"She risked her life for me? I could've destroyed you all?"

"Yes! Don't you realize that she cares for you? You're like a big sister to her. What more proof do you need?"

Tori sat quietly, pondering. "I hope she's not too shaken. I forgive her. I hope I would have had the courage to do the same for her!"

Snorting, the horse turned around. Her job was frustrating and it was hard to feel joyful. She walked quietly to look at the sleeping, tear-stained face of Annie, her partner. Red shook her mane and closed her eyes, trying to concentrate on the girl's thoughts. She picked up waves of guilt and concern. She felt guilty? Guilt was very hard to overcome. Red nudged her awake. "Wake up, Annie, we should go now."

Annie opened her eyes and sniffled, "I don't want to fight anymore with Tori." She grabbed onto the mare's neck and embraced her.

"Annie, you saved her. She lives because of you! Your sword dissolved the darkness surrounding her! Don't feel guilty! She doesn't understand why you took it upon yourself to do that, but she appreciates the second chance at life." Red nudged her cheek. Tears flowed from the girl's eyes like a waterfall. The noble red head rested lightly on her shoulder. "Cheer up. Let's get it together and rescue your sister."

Tori stood and approached her friend with her arms wide open. "Thank you for saving my life."

The two girls hugged fiercely until Red ordered, "Okay now, let's go!"

Annie and Tori mounted their horses, the young girl with the glowing sword, and Tori with her bird and cape. In the thinning moonlight, they galloped along the old forest path and toward the base of Mount Frost. Both were happy to be alive, and to be friends.

Annie had only slept an hour since the battle, and her eyes wanted to close. The soft chill to the air made the ride comfortable, the floral scent of the forest soothing. Gradually the trail led upwards and the air got thinner and crisper. The forest was not thinning, but thickening. Tall trees blocked the view of the mountain. The forest grew dark instead of light as the sun started to rise behind the mountains in the east. The light did not reach the forest floor. Bugs buzzed in the girls' ears and eyes, making it very uncomfortable.

"Darn bugs!" Tori hissed like a cat.

Each girl kept one hand in the air swatting the buzzing things and the other securely on the reins. Lone One and Red swished their tails and twitched their ears, also very annoyed.

After about an hour in the thick, buggy forest, Red reared. Her voice rang like a wind chime on hurricane winds. "That's it!" She lunged forward, nearly knocking her rider out of the saddle. Annie held on with her legs as Red galloped with all her might. Red pounded over the undergrowth, going through the brambles and thorny bushes on the forgotten path.

Lone One and Tori followed at their heels. The air was colder, and it started to chill noses and fingers. The trees were spaced more widely now. It was still a long way to go until the tree line, but the bugs had diminished due to the colder air. It was a welcome relief.

They slowed down to a walk and Red was breathing heavily. Annie took a deep breath. The air was crisp and smelled like she was the first person to breathe it in. A few creatures frolicked through the tangled weeds and plants while others burrowed under tree roots. Suddenly, Lone One reared so quickly that Tori tumbled off her back and landed on the dirt. She jumped up and grabbed the horse's reins before the he could gallop away.

Red twisted back to face the panicking horse, and Annie felt her tense up and say, "Mountain lion."

Lone One reared again and whinnied in fear. Tori remounted her and tried again to calm her down. Red sniffed the air. All Annie could smell was the fresh icy air and the pine of the forest.

Light golden brown shapes appeared from behind the bushes. There were four, and all had gleaming black eyes and sharp, deadly claws. They whispered to each other, sounding like the wind in the grass.

"Horse flesh," one hissed and licked its fangs. "I live for horse flesh. We will start right now, Canyon?"

Canyon's eyes sparkled with a dazzling blackness, and she bared her pearl-white fangs. Tensing her muscles, she growled, "No, I will start."

"I thought mountain lions lived alone," Annie asked, staring at the gleaming eyes fixed on her. Her hand slowly reached for her sword.

"In *your* world they do. Here on Mount Frost they travel in packs and hunt down travelers," Red replied, taking a defensive stance.

Canyon roared, "Your mistake has cost you your life!" She sprang toward Red and Annie raised her glowing sword. The girl swiped at the mountain lion's heart, but the sword just made a scratch. Its hide was thick and slick.

"Did you think a sword made from the pitiful power of the horse could defeat us?" Canyon sneered. "We are the horses' weakness!" The cat swiped at the mare's legs and Red fell down in a heap. The other creatures cornered Tori and Lone One. Lone One continued to rear and snort like a wild hog as Tori struggled to stay on.

Canyon screeched and lunged again at Red's noble head. Before the big cat landed to make the fatal bite, a howl and a flash of fur knocked it over. More black and silver shapes joined in at great speed with loud snarling and growling. The next thing the girls knew, the mountain lions were gone and a pack of wolves stood proudly before them. Their fur was bristled and their tongues hung out with saliva and blood dripping on the ground.

Red stumbled to her feet. "Thank you," she said gratefully. "You saved us."

A large black and silver wolf walked forward. "The mountain

lions of this area are enemies of our pack. They steal our pups and our food. They attack us at night when we are most vulnerable. We are always happy to save travelers from those cursed flea-bitten cats." The wolf spat on the ground and howled again triumphantly. "The minute we leave, the cat pack will return, so we shall accompany you to the tree-line."

As they walked along the worn path, a grateful Annie studied them. The wolves all had blue eyes flecked with green, except for the leader's eyes, which were flecked with red. In the light, their pelts shone with a fluorescent blue and violet sheen. They were twice the size of regular wolves on earth, and looked much faster and stronger. Their teeth gleamed like diamond razors and were sparkling white like pearls. When Annie looked down at the path, she saw thousands of faint mountain lion and wolf paw-prints indented into the dirt.

After about an hour of slowly walking upward, they finally saw a bright, sunny light coming from a tunnel of trees. A raven sat proudly upon a branch at the end of the path; its eyes glowed mysteriously as it watched the travelers pass from overhead.

"Rotuke, has there been any sign of the large cats?" The lead wolf gazed up at the bird, respect displayed in his eyes.

The midnight black feathers ruffled as the bird replied. "Yes, they are near your camp. You should hurry."

"Curse them! My pups are hidden there along with the she-wolves!"

Red looked conflicted as she watched the small party of wolves race toward the cliffs. The raven spoke again. "You'd best be on your way. You don't want to be caught up in another battle with those lions. Head up the mountain to the right. There is fog building there and it will give you cover." He then lifted his large wings and flew off in the direction the wolves had gone.

"Tori?" Annie said. "Are you thinking what I'm thinking?" Tori nodded as her horse also snorted in agreement. It didn't feel right to leave the wolves to fend for themselves after they had just saved their lives. They cantered off to help the wolves, the cold wind blowing in their faces.

———•——

The wolf leader could hardly see. The mountain fog had descended swiftly, making it almost impossible to find their way. Panic clouded his eyes. *What if I don't get there in time?* His pack whined nervously as they floundered around him. He anxiously sniffed the air and relief flooded him like a wave when he finally caught the scent of home. The happiness left swiftly, however, when another scent made its way into his nostrils. He could smell blood. With his heart slamming in his chest, he heard the chilling sounds of battle.

No! We must get there! The frost-covered ground scratched his hard, thick pads. He didn't notice the wind, the ice, and his painful paws. None of them did.

The sound of howling and growling wolves was getting closer and louder, mixing with the screeches of the mountain lions. The patrol thundered down a steep rocky cliff and plunged into the camp. The big cats were everywhere! The wolf leader thrust himself at the neck of a cat attacking one of his pups, the young one yipping in fear.

———•——

Red Mare galloped confidently over the hill, almost like she had traveled there before. Annie glanced behind and saw Tori pushing Lone One onward as if their lives depended on it. Heart's Song huddled in Tori's hood and shivered out a small whistle. The raven never looked back and didn't seem to notice as the group followed him toward camp.

Battle sounds filled their ears and Red's blood went cold listening to the mountain lions' screech. Wolves were howling and snarling and she could hear the terrified cries of the pups. The fog was growing thick—so thick that it started to cloud their vision as they burst down the ominous pathway between two cliff faces.

A large cat was guarding the entrance to ensure the wolves could not get away. It hissed in surprise as Red reared above it, bringing her hooves down on its back. Its mouse-dun pelt lay limply on the ground, its spinal cord severed by the impact. The mare gave a neigh of victory.

"Red, over there. Look!" Annie pointed toward an elevated opening in the cliff face where four mountain lions surrounded two she-wolves guarding the entrance. Red and Lone One launched themselves in that direction, scattering the cats as they went. The she-wolves, regaining the upper hand, snapped at the cats' throats. Two lions never had a chance to flee or breathe again.

"Toki", the leader yelled, "grab a pup. We might be able to escape to the emergency den now."

"Let me help." Annie dismounted and ran over to them. "I can carry a pup."

The wolves looked uncertain. Their fur bristled.

"Did you not see her on my back when we saved you from these four cats? You can trust her!" Red's voice boomed as she reared powerfully, kicking at another lion.

The wolves looked at each other and nodded in agreement to accept the girl's help. Annie followed as they crawled along the winding tunnel and entered a small chamber filled with four crying pups. The she-wolves each gently picked up a puppy by the scruff of the neck and crawled into a well hidden side-tunnel that was too small for a mountain lion to enter.

Annie picked up the remaining two pups and cradled them in her shirt. She crawled through the opening on one hand and two knees. It was damp and dark in the tunnel as the light faded. Soon it was so dark that she couldn't see the two wolves she held. Only small sniffles reached her ears. After a while of suffocating darkness, Annie began to wonder if the tunnel would ever end. The two she-wolves continued on, determined and silent. They were not interested in talking to the human.

Annie shook her head and spit as dirt kicked up from the wolves flew into her face. Her eyes were getting crusty from the dust. There was an uncomfortable silence from the pups and she started to get worried. Their eyes were shut and they stopped their pitiful little cries. Suddenly, light flooded into the tunnel, almost blinding her. Clear fresh air filled her lungs. They entered a small chamber with a small hole in the roof that let in a flood of light.

The two wolves gently dropped their pups on the ground, cushioning them on the dried reeds that they kept stored there. It was peaceful with no sounds of war or dying. There was only the sound of the soft wind gently tickling the icy grass above— and it was freezing! The hole didn't just let in light; it also let out the warmth.

Annie placed the two puppies next to their silver siblings and looked down at them, a male and a female. The female looked strong and lean, with a white pelt. One toe of her front paw was black. The male was brown with four black paws and a black and brown tail. Their colorings were beautiful and unusual.

The silvery she-wolf gave the white one a lick. "This is Yarka. It means snowbird in our language. The little male is Roark. It means fighter-of-great-strength." She seemed to smile in an endearing wolf way.

Annie asked, "Are they yours?"

"Yes, they are." The she-wolf gazed at the two silver pups with markings like her. "We haven't named these little rascals yet."

Annie smiled at the pups, and then looked up at the hole. "When will we know it's safe to go back?"

The other wolf spoke up. "When the battle is over, someone will fetch us. We dare not bring the pups back now that no one is guarding the den. Another lion might be waiting for us there. Those things are sinister and patient." She spat out the words like a piece of hair.

Annie shivered. That wolf scared her. *I wouldn't want to meet him alone in a dark, empty cave.* "I need to get back to my horse," Annie said out loud.

The wolf scowled, "That mare is not worth losing your life. She's probably dead now anyway."

Before she could protest, the other she-wolf's silky tail rested gently on Annie's leg, as if to calm her. "Now, that's no way to talk! Without her, two of my pups would be dead, and you would be, too!"

Annie felt a little better knowing the she-wolf Toki was on her side.

"Toki, that thing is a *human*. Humans don't care about the wolves. This one just wants a reward," the wolf responded indignantly.

"I do not! I truly just wanted to help," Annie cried out.

The angry she-wolf was about to launch herself at Annie when Toki slammed Harka to the ground.

"Enough! Harka! I don't want fighting in front of my pups! You know better than to attack someone who has helped us."

Harka backed down and put her tail between her legs. Toki was the alpha female and also her older sister. Harka had no power, and was only allowed to baby-sit and guard the pups.

"That's better", said Toki. "Wait! Listen. I hear someone coming!"

Harka listened and growled, "The pads are soft when they hit the ground, and it smells like a lion!"

Suddenly a long sandy paw reached down and struck the ash colored wolf on the head. Annie whipped around and saw a mountain lion on top of the hole scraping at the sides to make it bigger. She placed herself over the four pups and gently pushed them together. Harka didn't get up as Toki snarled and whipped around, clearly overwhelmed. Before Annie could stop her, Toki retreated down the tunnel, snarling as she went.

"No! Wait!" The girl screamed, but she stayed guarding the pups.

Roark and Yarka yelped at her in wolf language as the mountain lion from above clawed chunks of dirt off the roof. It snarled and swiped at Annie's face. The nauseating feeling of fear almost overwhelmed her as an out-stretched claw missed her by millimeters. Annie grabbed her sword and placed a wolf hair on the tip. It glowed golden for a second then flashed to white again.

"If you can't be defeated by the horse, maybe you'll will be defeated by the wolf!" she thought to herself. The sword glowed brightly as half of the roof started to cave in.

A sandy colored cougar waited behind the cloud of dust, tensing its muscles, ready to spring. "I told you," it snarled, showing its bloodstained teeth. "Horse swords do nothing!" The animal pounced, but Annie was ready. She held up the sword as the beast hit her. All went dark.

Chapter 7

Nothing. Her arm throbbed with pain and was hanging at an unusual angle. Her head ached and she felt something sticky and warm on her cheek. There was a metallic taste in her mouth. *Its blood!* Panic rushed through her. *Is it my blood or the cougar's?* something prodded her. *Is that the vengeful animal waiting to kill me off?* Something small and warm huddled close to her, making mewing sounds. Puppies! *Run puppies! Run!*

Her words came out in a whisper. She didn't have the strength to open her eyes, but her mind filled with pictures from dreams and reality. She could see her sister crying, huddled in a corner surrounded by shadows. She could see a cougar pouncing on her. She saw her friend, Red.

A vision appeared above her, looming larger as it came nearer. It was a figure bathed in a reddish glow. There stood Red Mare in her full glory, glowing like the desert sun. Joining her were three more horses who ran around Annie's unconscious body. Red walked regally forward and placed a small red flower in the girl's limp hand. It was a cactus-bloom. Annie closed her eyes tighter and then yanked them wide open. The dream was gone.

Annie opened her eyes looking at the limp face of a mountain lion. Its green-brown eyes were clouded and empty. Annie's right hand was still gripping her sword, which was covered in the cougar's blood. Her arm throbbing, she carefully turned her head to the left. The mountain lion's claw had managed to slice her arm when they fell. She had a cut on her head and was having a hard time breathing because the giant cat was lying on top of her!

"Human girl! You're alive." Toki rushed over, and with a grunt, pushed the dead cat off of her. The girl gasped for breath as soon as the thing was off her chest. In relief, she filled her lungs with cool, sweet air. Toki wagged her tail. Blood was on her claws and teeth.

"Are you hurt, too?" Annie asked.

The wolf vigorously shook her head no. "I killed a mountain lion, too!" she stated proudly. "I caught him by surprise inside the tunnel. He learned the hard way that mountain lions can't fight in tight spaces!"

"What about Harka and the pups? Annie moaned. "Are they all right?" It hurt to talk, and she felt uncomfortable and sticky with all the blood from the cougar on her.

Toki stopped wagging her tail, and the smile on her face disappeared. "Harka is dying," she said.

"Then we must help her!" Annie replied. All the pain and resentment she felt toward that bone-headed wolf left in a wave of concern as she sat up. She tried not to wince at the pain from her head and arm as she stumbled over to the ash-colored pelt of Harka. "Harka?" she asked. "Harka, can you hear me?"

Toki licked Harka's nose and whispered, "Come on, friend, speak! We want to see you open your eyes."

The ash colored face twitched a little. Slowly, one of her golden eyes opened.

Toki pushed her nose into her sister's neck fur, "You're going to be alright, Sis. The pups are safe and so are you."

Annie could tell that Toki wasn't at all convinced, that maybe she was trying to convince herself. She stroked Harka's fur with her unhurt arm and whispered, "I'll go get Red. Keep her warm, Toki."

Harka looked up in alarm, "No human! Don't waste your time. You won't get back fast enough. A storm is coming. I smell it. You'll get lost and freeze to death."

"I've got to try! We can't let you die." Annie got up and went over to the pups who were huddled on top of each other. Their blue-ice eyes were wide with fear, and they stumbled over to Annie on wobbly legs. She stroked them gently and said, "Can they howl yet?"

Toki nodded, "Yes, and quite loud, too!"

"Maybe if I call for Red, and you and the pups howl with me, someone would hear us." A cold wind blew dust and debris down from the former roof.

Toki agreed. "Or, you could go through the tunnels again, hoping there are no more wild cats. It would be faster."

"*Why didn't I think of that? It would be warmer and quicker— and more dangerous.* Annie nodded quickly, "Yes, that sounds like a better plan. I'll go as fast as I can." There was a tremendous need to hurry, and not just because Harka was dying. She knew the remains of the ceiling would soon topple down on top of them.

Annie scrabbled at the dirt and fell many times, getting dirt into her wounds. Her arm stung and her head throbbed, but she kept going. The tunnels seemed to have grown in size and it took longer to go through this time. The walls smelled of blood and death.

Will I ever get out of here? I need to hurry. Darn cougar! Why did I have to get wounded? I hope my cuts don't get infected.

It was even darker inside the tunnel than before. *Where did the light go?*

"And why is it so stuffy in here?" she said out loud. Panic pulsed through her. *Did the entrance to the den cave in, too?* She stumbled through the wider path on one hand and two knees. The fact that the tunnel was so long made her anxious. Then she hit a solid wall. Pain shot up her arm and her neck.

No, no, no, no ..."No!" she cried aloud. With her good arm she started to dig at the soil and rock in front of her, ripping her fingernails off in the process. "Help!" She yelled, doubting anyone could hear her through all the debris. "Help!" She called again, "The cave is collapsed and Harka is dying!" Her heart was beating like it wanted to break out of her chest; her breaths were quick and shallow as she clawed at the dirt with one hand.

"Human girl! Human girl!" a voice echoed excitedly off the walls of the tunnel.

Annie turned around and saw a small furry shape behind her. "Yarka?"

The pup ran over to her. "Rrrrrr we've rrr come to help." Her speech was still half growls and whines and hard to understand.

"We?"

"Rrrrrright here!" another voice chimed in.

"Roark!"

They barked and jumped upon her, their puppy breath sweet. Annie used her good arm to scoop them up and whispered, "I'm so glad to see you two! Okay now, who can howl the loudest?"

"I can," Yarka announced. Her talk was better then her brother's. *She must've have been listening to the grown-ups more*, Annie thought.

"Okay, Yarka. I want you to start howling. Roark, help me dig, big fella!"

"What, rrrrdo youggg want me to rrruf-say?"

Then it hit her, wolves say different things in their howls. "Say help! We're in here!"

After a few moments of thinking about it, Yarka started to howl. It wasn't crisp and ominous sounding, like an adult wolf's howl on a wintry night, but it was still loud and special.

Roark and Annie went to work digging at the wet dirt. Yarka's brother tried howling too, and did a pretty good job. Annie's arm started to throb and her neck stung when hit by dirt flung by the eager pup's paws. Feeling weaker and weaker, she started to slow down and couldn't scoop up as much dirt as her puppy friend. She had lost a lot of blood and felt so tired. She blinked, and fell back unconscious.

———·———

Red jumped up and flicked her ears. She heard something behind the wall of dirt. They had driven the mountain lions out, but the dirty creatures collapsed the entrance to the den before running away.

The leader of the wolf pack recognized the howl. "That's Yarka!"

"They're alive!" Red reared, showing off her full might. "Quick! Start digging!"

The wolves jumped up and, despite their injuries, put their full power into digging out the pups. Red couldn't do much more than paw at the dirt, but Tori could. She dismounted and joined in the scramble. The soil thinned and soon a little head poked out. It was brown with black across its muzzle and ears.

"Roark!" The leader helped dig him from the soil and then snatched him up by the scruff of his neck. The pup giggled.

"Daddy!" Yarka jumped out and almost knocked both of them over.

Red Mare smelled blood, human blood. "Everybody stand back," she ordered.

The wolves backed away as she reared and came down hard, pushing her weight onto her front hooves, slamming herself at the dirt. It crumbled in a heap and the opening was made wider. There was Annie, unconscious on the floor with large wounds on her arm and head.

"Quick! Help me get her out!"

Two wolves gently dragged her out.

"Annie!" She didn't move. "Annie!" The mare lay down beside her and rested her noble head on the young girl's chest. She matched her breathing to the girl, and soon found herself drifting off into oblivion. In the dream she knew what to do. She galloped forward, hooves glowing with light. She saw a shape on the ground and it was Annie. She reared and yelled, "Four Hooves! Heal!"

Three ghostly horse shapes galloped around them, each whispering in ghost speech. The mare saw a cactus flower and gently plucked it from the earth, placing it in Annie's limp hand. Red awoke and jumped up as Annie started to wake. She smiled down at her.

The girl opened her eyes and gasped, "Harka is dying. They need our help. Hurry!" Hearing this, the wolf leader gathered five warrior wolves and charged into the tunnel.

"Red, they need you, too," Annie whispered.

"You need me more, little girl. You have nasty wounds on your head and arm. Harka can wait. I'll get to her in time."

"Red, how do you heal?" Annie asked painfully.

"I can't tell you now, but someday I will. You'll know everything at the right time."

Heart's Song chirped and landed on Annie's shoulder. Tori walked over and smiled down at Annie. "We beat those flea-bitten bags of fur."

"Funny, I didn't see Canyon anywhere." the red mare said shaking her long mane. "She doesn't give up *that* easily."

"Canyon's dead!" Annie blurted out. "Canyon is dead and I killed her!"

The wolves around her yelped in surprise and backed away in respect. Someone who could defeat the most dangerous mountain lion of all was to be feared.

Red was dumbfounded, "What? How?"

"I used my sword. By placing a wolf hair on it, I gave it a great power."

"Wolf and horse... hmmmm, Annie, what wolf hair did you use? What color was it?" Red asked.

"I think it belonged to Harka. It was ash-black," she said.

Red froze and stood staring into the distance, as if looking at something far away and out of reach.

"Red? What's wrong?"

"After I help Harka, we must leave. Quickly." Saying that, she galloped away.

———

Tori sat with Annie the whole night waiting for the patrol to return. They talked about what had happened after Annie left. Tori and Lone One kept guard of the camp entrance and left no opening where a mountain lion could escape.

"I'm surprised that you killed Canyon. That dirty feline almost killed all of us."

"Not as surprised as I was," Annie replied.

The night was cold and they huddled together in the back of the wolf den. Snow was piling at the entrance, glittering like diamonds in the moonlight. The sky was black and the wind was blowing snow. Tori stroked Heart's Song as the robin huddled closer to keep warm. Lone One was sleeping peacefully with both humans resting against her back. After sharing some shriveled apples, they all fell asleep.

Annie woke before the sun rose. The storm was still blowing and growing. Tori began to stir and the wolves yawned, stretched, and shook themselves of sleep. A faint sound of howling broke the silence as the canines stormed outside, snow and wind whipping at their fur. They gathered with white flakes piling on their backs and muzzles. Annie held her arms against her body and shivered. She loved the cold, but not when it bit into her skin. The wolves walked over to the front of the cave and, as the wind howled, they heard a wolf howl answer in return.

"They've come back!" Annie cried with relief.

Red and grey figures came into view and slowly made their way down the sides of the cliff. The wolf leader followed with his mate, Toki. Each held a pup in the jaw, and set them down outside the cave. Their tails were lowered.

Annie could not see Harka. "Red?"

The horse stood sadly in the snow, the wind blowing her mane, swishing her tail around like reeds. Her head was hanging low.

One look confirmed what she feared. Harka was dead. Toki looked up at the stormy sky and howled a mournful tune. The others joined in and, together, they all grieved over Harka's death.

Chapter 8

The wind blew at them from all sides. "Drat! I hate snow!" the mountain lion cried out to the sky. Everywhere she turned it was white. It felt like she had walked into another dimension.

Suddenly, small, slithering things started to melt out of the snow.

"Toblins," the cougar muttered. *Wonderful,* he thought with sarcasm. The lions shared one enemy with the wolves: Toblins. They were gruesome and evil. Every year on a special day, the Toblins went into another world and captured a victim to rip apart. They would then burn the remaining parts and send them tumbling down the mountain. The cat shivered; they didn't just take one victim, but two. Sometimes more if they felt like it. Canyon was afraid she would be next.

"Whhoo daresss to tresspasssss into our part of the mountain?" they all whispered at once.

"It is I," she stated boldly, "the great leader of the Mountain Lions, Canyon."

"Nooooo, it can't be *you.* We saw your quarrel with the human girl."

Canyon stuck out her chest, revealing a large gash over her heart. "I'm a mountain lion and mountain lions don't have hearts." A shadow passed over her eyes. "I once did, but I have nine lives. When you lose your first life, you also lose your heart. Without a heart, you are invincible."

"Nooooo, that can't beeee, fire and claws are all it takes." They started to approach from all sides.

"Touch me and you'll wish you hadn't!"

"Brave little kitty," they said in unison, "To bad you'll die in two days."

"No!" Canyon snarled, glaring at each one of them. "You won't take me alive!"

"Yes, we will." One slithered forward. "Oh, yes, we will."

Yet another Toblin jumped from behind and hit Canyon on the head. She fell to the ground, slipping into unconsciousness. The last words she heard were, "Fire and claws, fire and claws. FIRE AND CLAWS!"

"How long will it take to get to the Toblins' lair?" Annie said, breathing hard.

"About two days," Red replied as they climbed the slope. Because of the snow, the world around them was white.

"I sure hope we get off this mountain in two days," Tori said. She held Heart's Song in her hand and covered him with her sleeve. The robin wasn't doing well since the race to warn Red and Annie of the trap. Tori stroked him soothingly and said, "I can't see anything ahead."

"*I can,*" a voice said in the wind.

"*Father? Is that you?*"

"*Yes. You're nearing a dangerous spot, my dear, a very disturbing spot. Be wary, and be safe.*"

"*I will Father, I will.*"

"*I must be leaving now, child, but I am with you in spirit.*"

"*Wait, Father. Heart's Song is not well. He doesn't sing or fly anymore. Will you help him?*"

"*His time is coming my dear. There is nothing I can do.*"

"*So you are saying he'll die?*"

"*Yes, as soon as you leave the mountain.*"

"*Two days?*"

"*Yes, two days. I'm sorry for your loss. I must go now.*"

A sickening feeling engulfed Tori. *Heart's Song only has two days to live? My sweet little bird?* "Annie?" she called. "Red?"

They stopped and turned around. "What is it Tori."

"Heart's Song is dying." A tear rolled down her cheek.

"What? Oh no!" Annie's eyes filled with tears, "Is there anything we can do?" Annie looked at Red with pleading eyes.

Red solemnly shook her head, nodded respectfully to Tori, and walked away.

"Red, can't you do something?" Annie called after her. "We all love that little robin. Use your powers and heal her!"

"No. The bird's time has come. There is nothing I can do," she said sadly.

Annie couldn't help but wonder why Red didn't bother to help the little bird. After all, didn't the mare help her? How does she know when someone's time has come? Annie put her arms around Tori and held her as she sobbed.

———

Red was grumpy and tried to climb at a brisk trot, but kept sliding. The mountain was getting steep and slick, and it was hard for Red's hooves to grip anything. They walked for thirty more freezing minutes before the mare finally stopped and said, "You two, get something to eat."

Annie glanced at Tori, who had been silent for half a day now.

They sat beside each other and pulled some jerky from their saddlebags. The jerky was hard, frozen, and old. It was bland and tasted terrible. It made Annie's mouth feel colder than it did already, but they had to eat something.

"Here, Red, eat this," Annie said, throwing her an apple. The cold had preserved the last two apples. She tossed the second one to Tori, who fed it to Lone One.

But the red mare shook her head at the apple. "No. We'll need it after we rescue your sister."

"Come on, you need your strength too. I mean, you're carrying me and climbing a mountain at the same time. You need the energy."

Red just shook her head again, so Annie reluctantly put it back into the bag. *You can lead a horse to water, but you can't make it drink!*

Tori sniffed and urged her horse onward. Red followed, her head hanging lower than usual. Annie was growing worried about her horse and friend. One had a dying pet and the other seemed to be dying! Her arm and neck throbbed, making the ride miserable. Nobody seemed happy. *Why should we be?* Annie asked herself. *We're in the snow, we're cold, and someone is dying. I'm closer to finding my sister, but also closer to those slithering serpents. This is miserable!*

They rode for another ten minutes when suddenly Red and Lone One stopped in unison.

"What's wrong?" Annie asked.

"There is a steep drop-off one step away," Red snorted loudly, and it came back as a faint echo.

The snow cleared just enough for Annie to see the dark rocky outline of a crevice. She couldn't see the bottom. On the other side lay a figure. It was still except for a twitch of the tail.

"There is a body on the other side. I think it may still be alive. We need to help." Red said.

How will we cross?" Annie asked.

"Jump," Red said.

"How will Tori and Lone One jump across?"

"They won't. They'll stay here until we get back."

Annie looked at Tori, who simply shrugged. "That's alright. Go. I'll wait for you here."

"Okay then, Red. Let's go. I'm ready," Annie said.

The mare nodded and tensed her muscles, ready to jump. She backed up five steps, then sprang into a dead-out gallop and glided into the air. Annie felt like she was flying as the mare pushed off and sliced through the air.

They landed inches away from the edge and Annie dismounted and ran to the figure. Red followed behind cautiously.

The body on the ground was a brown cougar with a maimed face and body. It looked as if fire had been set to one side of his body and he was left to die. The cat had lost an eye and half an ear. The burn wound stretched down one leg and across his side. Annie wanted to scream, but the fear of attracting those who had done this was greater than the impulse to scream.

Red stared down at the cougar with pity as he looked up at her with his good eye. "You've come to finish me off?" His voice was raspy. His black gaze then pointed straight at Annie. She felt uneasy and took another step back.

"Cougar, what happened to you?" Red asked.

He coughed and choked on his blood. "Toblins captured us, but we fought. They took Canyon away. They'll start The Ceremony in one day. We tried to stop them but they used fire. I think I'm the only other one alive besides our leader." He coughed again and found it harder to breathe.

Panic rushed through Annie like a cobras' poison. "Canyon? I thought I killed her!"

The cougar smirked, "Ha! You never killed her. She has nine-lives and that was just her first life."

"Then The Ceremony won't kill her, either. Right? What is this 'Ceremony' anyway?"

The cougar looked up at her and said in a raspy voice, "Fire and claws will kill the most powerful."

Then his eyes rolled back in his head and he had a seizure. The shaking brought his ravaged body too close to the edge for Annie or Red to prevent him from falling over into the black abyss. It was many seconds before they heard the thud below.

"So, what is this 'Ceremony?'" Annie had been anxious to know ever since they left the cliff edge.

Red tensed, then answered. "Once, every year on a night of no moon, the Toblins go to another world and gather victims to sacrifice. Two years ago, they found their way to Earth and developed a taste for humans. If you've ever wondered why someone disappears and is never seen again, Toblins are the culprits. They believe killing innocent lives once a year will give them more power. They kill with fire and claws, and then they take the maimed, burnt bodies and eat them. Afterwards they lay dormant in a ceremony room for two months. When they wake, they are bigger, stronger, and more vicious. Every year they get more powerful and soon they will be unstoppable. They have captured Canyon and your sister Louise for this very reason."

Fear froze her insides. *My sister is going to be killed in this gruesome way? We need to get there now!*

"These creatures have been doing this for years and you didn't stop them? Why is now any different?"

"They haven't been a threat until now. They are getting so powerful they are now threatening the lives of our world. If they can manage to take over this world, they will take over your world next."

"They must've been pretty powerful last year. Why didn't you stop them then?"

Red sighed. "We had to wait until the time was right. There is a prophecy about a girl and the Four Hooves. We believe that you and your sister are going to make that prophecy come true."

"Us?"

"You."

Annie pondered silently as she rode. *Me? A part of a prophecy? That can't be true!* Then another question came to mind. "Who are the Four Hooves?"

Red shook her mane. *Why did she have to ask so many questions?* "The Four Hooves is a group of four horses, each with a special power, and each with a special purpose. I am a part of that group. We're the guardians of this world."

"Oh," Annie said, pretending to understand.

They walked on in silence for a bit. The snow was piled up almost to Red Mare's shoulders. It was hard to walk and Red wished she had the legs of a moose.

"Wasn't that story just *wonderful?*" a slithery voice said in the frozen whiteness.

"Yessss, it was!" The second voice seemed to be right in front of them.

"Annie! They found us!" Red reared so suddenly she seemed to hit the sky with her hooves. Red noticed the small wooden door barely visible under a rock to the right.

"Annie, quick! Run for that door by the rock!" Your sister will be in there. I'll meet you after I take care of this."

Obeying, she slipped off of Red and rested her hand on the hilt of her sword.

"Brave little girlllll." one creature said.

"Yessss, she isss." another one whispered.

A slithering figure glided toward the girl, but Red kicked it away. The attackers then turned their attention to the mare instead, and Annie ran toward the rock. She got down on her stomach and slipped through the doorway without being noticed.

Chapter 9

The tunnel was wide and smelled of death and decay. Torches hung on the walls, creating menacing shadows. Annie's thoughts returned to the dying cougar and the Ceremony. She could smell something cooking in the distance. Quickly, she pushed away the thought of bloody cougars and humans in a boiling pot. All thoughts of being hungry vanished as she quietly made her way downward. She heard murmurs and slithery voices come from a doorway up ahead. Peeking in, she saw a large assembly of Toblins listening to one of their own standing at a podium. It was speaking in a language Annie didn't understand. She dashed past the doorway and ran as fast and as quietly as she could. Hoping that no one saw her, she slipped past an armory and a kitchen.

The tunnels went down and down, and soon she came to a split. One hallway to the right was lit with many torches and had many doorways. The other was dark and barely had any light at all. The only door was at the end of the dark hall. Deciding to take the less populated path, Annie veered to the left. It was dark and stuffy and it felt like the air was smothering her.

Sneaking along the wall she came to a stone door that had claw marks all over it. Pushing open the door, Annie saw a room lit with torches. On the ground lay a half-conscious mountain lion. Her pelt was light gold and familiar.

Annie looked closer. "Canyon?"

The cat turned her head to at look the girl. "So, we meet again."

The cougar's voice was weak, hardly above a whisper. Annie couldn't help but feel sorry for her.

"I'll help get you out of here. But first, where is my sister?"

"The little human girl? She's in the next room."

Annie walked over to a stone door. The sound of chains clanged as the lion tried to stand, but fell back to the floor. Annie pushed open the door and stepped into a room with one torch on the wall. A figure lay huddled in the corner with a Toblin standing guard.

Annie raised her sword that began to glow brightly against the shadows.

"Release her."

The thing turned and grinned a snake-like smile.

"You should stay for our Ceremony! I'm sure you'll be very welcome—and delicious."

"I've come for my sister! Release her at once"

The huddled figure turned at the sound of Annie's voice.

"Annie!" Louise's face brightened. "Annie, you're here!"

"Yes, and I'm going to set you free. "Release her, I said!"

The Toblin took a knife and waved it about. "Try me human."

Annie lunged and landed a blow on the arm that held the knife. It screeched as the knife dropped and she kicked it across the floor.

"Let my sister go." Annie clenched her teeth so hard it hurt; anger was boiling inside her like a volcano. She held the sword point against its neck.

"Would you really do that?" it asked with a grim smile.

"Yes, I would. Now free her."

"Are you sure?"

He's stalling, she thought. He might have signaled someone.

Annie rammed the sword into its body and the Toblin died instantly, the grin never leaving its face.

They need to get out quickly! Annie rushed over and picked Louise off the floor, dragging her out. The young girl was weak and could barely walk. Annie ran to the dead Toblin and grabbed the keys from around its neck. She then ran back to the mountain lion and opened her chains. Canyon warily got up and shook her sore back. Her eyes looked grateful as she followed them out.

Together they ran through the door and into the hallway. A Toblin was coming for shift change, and he stopped when he saw the trio.

Canyon stepped protectively in front of the girls as the monster loaded a bow and arrow. The cougar walked straight toward it, staring at it with her fierce eyes. The creature started to shiver and flinch as they stood face to face. Annie watched in amazement as the lion lifted a paw and slammed the monster to the ground. It was over after one ferocious bite to its throat.

Annie's sister clung to her hand as the three glided past the kitchen and the armory. The meeting was still in session, though it appeared as if the group was about to adjourn. The girls and the cougar ran even faster, for fear that the monsters would see them when they were dismissed.

Louise was breathing hard and holding her cramping sides. She stumbled and fell to the ground and dragged Annie down with her. Sharp pain pierced her leg as her sister landed on it awkwardly.

"Ahrg!" Annie grunted. Her arm still ached badly.

Canyon heard her cry of pain and skidded to a halt. "Get up, we don't have much time," she said impatiently.

Annie tried to get up but it hurt too much. Louise tried to help her but she was too small and weak to be much aid.

Canyon heard a shout from far off and smelled fire being kindled. "They've found out we're gone," she warned.

"Go without me, then. My mission is done," Annie said, tears welling in her eyes. She would not let her sister and friend die because of her.

"No, we are not leaving you," Canyon said firmly. "I have an idea!" he said. "You two, get onto my back."

They both looked at the cat, dumbfounded. The shouts from behind were coming closer.

"Can you carry two people?" Annie asked nervously.

"Come *on!* I'm a cougar and have eight more lives. Of course I can. Now get on my back!"

The two girls struggled onto the tall lion and held on tight as she zoomed forward in a gallop-jump-run. They swayed with the cougar's movements and rode with ease. The entrance was just ahead but the shouts were getting louder.

"Run, Canyon, run!" Annie screamed.

They came to the door and Canyon skidded to a halt, almost throwing the girls off.

"Louise, open the door," Annie ordered, still in pain.

Her sister hopped off and ran to the wooden door with the carvings. She heaved it open and sprinted back onto Canyon. As they left, Annie picked up one of the torches and slammed the door shut before setting fire to it.

They made it outside as the sun was coming up behind the far-off mountains. Storm clouds covered almost all except the tallest peaks. The trio was buffeted with strong winds and icy snowflakes. Canyon slipped and made a few unstable sidesteps before gaining traction.

"Hold on!" she called and glided through the air with her unique gallop-jump-run.

———————

The wind made their cheeks and noses turn red, and the sharp air hurt their teeth. Annie looked around and saw no sign of Red. *Did they capture her?* She told herself no, and tried to concentrate on riding the cougar. Louise was nearly choking her, the little girl's hands holding tight around her neck. Canyon was starting to get tired, so Annie suggested that they slow a bit.

"No, there is a crevice ahead and I must be going at full speed in order to get across!"

"You won't make it if you are too tired to jump!"

"I will. I won't let you fall, but you must hold on tight! Now!"

Through the white and grey, Annie could barely see the dark space where the deep gash in the mountain went down. She shivered, remembering the cougar falling off into the blackness.

As they built up speed Annie told her, "One of your mountain lion friends fell off this crevice."

"Was he dark brown with an unusual black marking above the eyes?"

She remembered that the lion had dark brown and grey in his fur. It had been too snowy to see his full face.

"I didn't see his eyes, but he had grey and brown in his pelt."

Canyon stumbled in grief. "No! That was Smokey!" Sadness consumed her. "He was my best friend. He saved my life once."

"I'm sorry," Annie said sadly.

They were quiet as they neared the crevice. Annie could feel the mountain lion start to tense her muscles and then—suddenly—they flew through the air and landed onto the other side of the cliff. They stumbled and tumbled into a pile of snow.

"Are you two alright?" Canyon mumbled.

"Yes," they shivered in unison. "Nice jump!"

"Tori should be around here somewhere."

"Who?" Louise and Canyon looked at Annie with questioning looks.

"Tori is a friend of mine. Canyon, she could give Louise a ride so that you wouldn't have to carry both of us."

"Lucky me," Canyon grumbled. Once again, the girls climbed back onto the cougar's back as she walked along the cliff edge. After several minutes they saw a dark, tall shape in the distance. They ambled forward and came face to face with Lone One. The horse reared with fear and backed away as they came closer into view.

"Annie?" Tori looked past her horse's head. "Is that *you*?"

"Yes, don't be afraid. I'm with Canyon and my sister Louise," Annie reassured her.

"I… I thought you were dead," Tori said, feeling confused.

Confusion filled Annie, too. "Dead? Why would you thin that?"

"I saw Red walking back alone. She didn't see me and when I tried to follow, she just disappeared out of sight. Since you weren't with her, I thought the worst."

"You mean she just abandoned us? Me? While I was in the Toblins' lair, she just *left*?"

"I don't know why she left. I just saw what I saw."

Red Mare left me? How could she? I thought we were here to rescue my sister together! What about the prophecy?

Red made her way slowly up the mountain. It was a clear night and the rocks seemed to glow with moonlight. The mare passed a small pool that held the reflection of the orb on its surface. Stopping, she gazed into it and saw the image change into a snowy scene. She saw Annie and Louise sitting upon Canyon as they were talking to Tori. Red saw Annie flinch in surprise. *She knows I left her.* The horse heard her friend's mind say, *"Red Mare left me? How could she? I thought we were here to rescue my sister together!"*

"I don't know how to make you understand, Annie," whispered Red to the pool.

The image in the water changed again and the horse saw a cave filled with pools of acid. There were statues of monsters everywhere. *The place in my dreams!* A large, dark figure of a cat sat gazing into the green, glowing acid. She heard him think, *I lost a valuable servant. Canyon is a traitor! His* words were filled with disgust. Red peered closer. *What is he doing now?*

An army of shadows surrounded the cat, the creatures talking in low whispers. Red couldn't hear what they were saying but she could hear their thoughts. Hatred and anger boiled through her mind as she listened to their plans of blood, swords, revenge and death. *War! They are planning a war! she thought. What would happen to our beautiful world if the shadow army took over? I have to warn Sunrise!*

As Red reared and turned, a small pebble bounced off her hoof and into the water, rippling the image. The glowing eyes of the shadowy cat fixed his gaze on Red. If something disturbed the dream pool's surface, the people or animals being watched would know. They could communicate through the water.

Red saw the glowing eyes looking at her. "Looks like we have ourselves a little snoop," said the image of the cat in the pool. Beware, Red Mare! Once you are done with tonight's duties, you'll need to be watching your back. The shadow army will be upon you before your next breath."

The image faded and the mare, shaking with fright, walked slowly up the mountain. She reached the top in a few moments and found Sunrise waiting. He glowed with the light of the rising sun, but he had a frown on his face.

"Red Mare!" Sunrise yelled.

She cringed before his voice. "I'm here, Sunrise, and I carry one last urgent message."

"I already know! You let Him know you were watching him right after you gathered that important information! You know better than that!"

She bowed her head in shame, and even though he hadn't said the words, she knew it was time for her to lose her powers.

Crimson mist surrounded her hooves as Sunrise stared down at her.

"Red Mare, every Four Hooves member leaves. You have been on the team long enough and have fulfilled your destiny. You have led them into battle and you have used your joyful powers to heal the sick and wounded. You saved this world once in the last Great Battle with the shadow army, but unfortunately, for you and the world, you will not fight another."

Red bowed her head. Not with shame, but with dignity and humility. She recalled those days when the land was new and she brought peace and joy into the world. She was responsible for saving many lives. She had been the leader of the Four Hooves who appeared before her now—not as ghosts, but as real horses. They lined up in a row to her right. There was a tall, storm colored stallion, a pure white colt, and a beautiful bay mare.

The stormy stallion lifted his head and said, "I am Strength!"

The colt lifted his head in a similar fashion and decreed, "I am Truth!"

The mare gazed calmly into Red's eyes before lifting her head saying, "I am Courage!"

Then, they all bowed their heads in unison to honor her—their leader, friend, and comrade.

Red reared, showing off her full might. "I am Joy!" she declared.

The stars seemed to shine brighter as the four great horses reared as one, pawing the ground, and shaking it like thunder.

Sunrise silenced the horses' cries and neighs with a loud shout. They waited for him to speak.

"Horses of the Four Hooves, your leader and friend will be leaving your ranks. She has done good work with you, and, of course, the team won't be the same without her. Someday each of you will also leave the team and go on your own journey. It is time to say your goodbyes and leave. Red Mare must make her last steps alone."

The stallion and colt walked to Red Mare and nodded their heads in unison. They turned and jumped into the air, vanishing in the process. The bay mare then walked up and flicked her black tail.

"Goodbye, sister. I'll miss you." Red's sister rubbed her pink nose against her neck. "One day soon we will share a dandelion patch together again in our forest home." They nickered and parted. "Have Courage!" the bay said and vanished.

"Have Joy," Red Mare replied to the wind.

Sunrise led her over to a tunnel and motioned for her to enter. He followed her through the dark entrance. Red closed her eyes; she hated places where she couldn't see the sky. When she sensed light through her closed lids, she opened them and saw a cave of crystals. A small waterfall ran over one wall and made a pool of turquoise water. The stars shone brightly above.

She looked at Sunrise who said gently, "As you walk along this path, your powers will gradually fade until you are a normal horse once again. You will still be able to talk, but you will not be able to heal. You may go find Annie if you wish, but you'll have to be more careful. We'll miss you on the team, but there will be another one to take your place. I must warn you, however, he who leads the Shadow Army has ordered his minions to look for you. You won't be able to break out of their trances and traps as easily as before. You will be vulnerable to them."

Red nodded in understanding. "I will be careful. I will do my best to make the world a better place, even without powers or my partners by my side."

"Good, my faithful servant. Now go, and peace be with you." Sunrise swished his tail and left the cave of crystals and stars, disappearing into the mist.

Red saw that the path ahead was long and dark, but she couldn't sense any danger. She drank deeply from the waterfall fed pool. A sense of calm filled her body, along with the satisfaction of knowing that she had done her best on her journey up to now. The red mist around her hooves started to fade to a light pink as she made her way down the trail to her new life. Not all of it faded away, however. Some of the power seemed to linger.

Chapter 10

Annie sat gloomily upon Canyon's back. It had been three hours since the rescue of her sister and they were all so tired they could hardly keep their eyes open. Soon, however, they arrived at the wolf territory in no-mans land. Knowing they'd be safe, they collapsed and fell asleep.

———

Annie dreamed. She was at an entrance guarded by two fearsome statues that seemed to watch her every step. She ran past them into a large cavern. It was filled with even more statues of monsters. Green, glowing acid formed bubbling pools around a dark throne. Shadow figures walked around her but they didn't seem to notice her. A large shape was mumbling something harsh in the corner. He was gazing into the glowing acid and she heard him speak about Canyon being a traitor.

Is he saying that my friend is a traitor?

Suddenly, a shadow army appeared out of nowhere. Annie nervously stood amongst them, listening to their snickers and laughs of hatred. The large shape had eyes as green as the acid in the pools.

"Army of Shadow!" he called out, showing black and bloody fangs. "The time has come. Red Mare is no longer a part of the Four Hooves. We will strike on the night of no moon!" Cheers rose from the circle of shadow figures until the large cat-like figure silenced them with a wicked grin. "For those of you who are too stupid to know when that is, it's tomorrow!"

They all cheered again and this time he let them calm down by themselves before saying, "When Red Mare gets out of the Tunnel of Crystals and Stars, she will have no power! There will be no wolves and no human girls to stand in our way. I will be the one to kill that hay bag!"

Annie gasped and felt faint. *Kill Red? No more powers? What does he mean?*

"First, we will storm out of the crater of Mount Ablaze and wipe out any forces that stand in our way. We will then raid Arfag, crumble Framabal Town, and destroy the harbor. We will crush the horse world, along with Sunrise! The Kingdom of Stars will fall!"

The evil creatures laughed and cursed the name Sunrise and Red Mare. Annie huddled in the corner of the cave, but the cat noticed her. "Well, it looks like we have ourselves a little snoop." With a loud roar, it jumped on her. She screamed as it pinned her to the ground with a paw bigger than her whole body. "This is the human girl who destroyed one of my warriors. Tell me, you pathetic human, do you want to see your dear little horsy again?"

For the first time Annie hated the word horse. When she thought of horses now, she thought of Red and how she had abandoned her to the Toblins. She shook her head and the shadowy mountain lion saw the truth in her eyes.

"My my, it looks like this little hero holds hatred in her heart."

The shadow figures laughed and shouted until he silenced them with a roar.

"Tell me little girl, what did that horse do to you?"

She whispered, "She left me to the mercy of the Toblins."

The cat sneered, "Your little 'friend' left you for the Toblins? Not much of a friend now is she? More like a *traitor?*" The army laughed and jeered until the cougar roared again.

"If you see that lying, ungrateful equine again, I think you should show her how you feel about being betrayed. You have her knife, don't you? Listen to your hatred, human, and let it guide you. It will make you free!"

Annie struggled under his weight. She knew what he said was wrong; she needed to save Red... Didn't she? Red could just fend for herself, couldn't she? Feeling conflicted, Annie tried to kick at his pads, but the cat only laughed.

"Getting defiant, are you? Remember what I said. Thrive on your hatred, grow in it, and let it guide you."

Annie dreamed on.

Red galloped over the grass; it was so beautiful. The mountains were green, the sky was blue, and the dew made her hooves pleasantly cold. *I'm running at full speed again to save my world.*

She knew where Annie would go. She would leave Mount Frost and make her way to the harbor, where she would get a ride back to town. From there she would leisurely make her way back to Arfag. *How will I get to Mount Frost and Arfag in one day and then fight for the world of horses? I'll need help.*

Thundering across the wet, cold meadow, the ground shook and she held her head high. Power pulsed through her as she sped across the large, emerald green field. Red was going to Talon Peak, so named because of its shape. The peak held the highest bird population in her world, and she knew she would find help there.

The ground rose, and soon she was climbing a smooth mountain trail shielded by a thick canopy of trees. Forest birds sang their songs and went about their business as they watched the mare gallop by.

Red snorted and smelled the faint scent of feathers, nests, and freshly killed prey. Upon these cliffs and in the cracks of Talon Peak, many kingdoms of birds reigned. She would have to climb to the top of the mountain to reach the birds she wanted. As she neared a rocky wall, she slowed to a nervous halt. The wall stretched upward so steeply, no mortal horse could climb it. "Great Sunrise! How can I get up there?" she shouted.

As she stood puzzled, her jaw slightly ajar, a golden flash caught her eye. She turned around to look and saw a golden eagle perched upon a jagged rock. It preened its feathers and gazed calmly at her with eyes like golden fire.

"Greetings, Golden Eagle of the Sun," Red said in a formal greeting.

The bird stared at her and lifted its great wings off of its sides. Its wingspan was twice as long as Red and held enough power to blow a newborn foal away. It studied her with one eye before speaking.

"Greeting mare of red, protector of birds. What is your business here?"

Red was about to answer when black shapes stormed from the bushes and swept around them. The eagle screeched and flapped his wings. Red stood warily as the shadows stopped and assumed shapes of black eagles.

"We're here, Red Mare," the voices surrounding them announced. "He wants you now!"

"Mare, what are they talking about, did you summon them?" the eagle asked.

"They want to destroy me, and take over our world. I came here to ask for your help, Golden Eagle of the Sun."

"Those pathetic winged things can't help you now, mare; we are growing in power. Soon we will break out and storm across this world and destroy the horses and everyone else that stands in our way. You need not bother gathering allies or armies. It's useless! We'll smash them until no one is left standing!"

The eagle's eyes blazed with a golden fire. Red watched as the bird lifted up into the air and dove into the shadowy bunch. The next thing she knew, the shapes dissolved into smoke. The eagle sat in their place, glaring at the others who remained.

"Anyone *else?*"

Those who remained transformed into horses and galloped away.

"Those things are going to take over this world?" he asked.

"Don't underestimate them," Red said. "They're powerful. I was once able to defeat them, but I cannot anymore."

"And that's why you need our help?"

"From any and every bird that is willing."

The eagle spread his mighty wings and took off. After a few moments, Red could barely see him in the distance. *Wow, he's a fast flyer!*

The leader of the birds returned a few minutes later. He alighted next to the mare and said, "They want to hear you speak."

Overhead, a huge shadow fell on her face as a cloud of golden eagles blocked out the sun and filled the trees around them. They were silent as they studied her.

"Great Golden Eagles of the Sun Kingdom," Red began. "A threat has come upon the land. The Great Cougar of the Cave has planned an invasion to conquer our world. Anything that stands in his way will be destroyed. Alone we cannot fight him, but if we join together, we can defeat him and keep our lives safe."

The largest of the eagles spoke. "What about the Toblins and the prophecy about the two girls?"

"They have succeeded in their first quest, and now it is time for us to help them to save our world. I have traveled with one of the girls. She is strong-willed and capable. If you agree to help, gather every bird willing to fight! We must gather an army of our neighbors and encourage them to fight for the fate of our world!"

The largest eagle spoke up again. "Where is this going to take place?"

"Arfag and the Castle," Red replied.

The eagle stared at her and then closed his eyes for a moment and sighed before speaking. Reluctantly, he said, "We will join you. If what Golden Fire says is true, then this shadow army you talk of is a threat. And the Bird Kingdoms annihilate threats!"

The golden eagles cheered and cawed and were about to take off when Red called, "Wait! The invaders plan to attack tonight when there will be no moon to help us see them. Be prepared and get there at noon. You also need to send at least four eagles to Mount

Frost and pick up the two girls from the prophecy and their companions as well. Try to round up some wolves too. Wolves can defeat cougars."

The eagle nodded in agreement and cawed out orders. Five eagles flew off in the direction of the snowy mountain. Golden Fire stayed perched next to Red.

"I'll go with you to Arfag. We'll have to warn the people of the coming threat and get them to help us."

The mare gratefully nodded as the eagle lifted his massive wings and flew off into the sky.

Chapter 11

Annie glumly rode upon the cougar's back, the warm breath from the beast's nose curled like dragon smoke in the chilly air. She still did not understand why Red would leave her. And why would she have a dream that felt so real? The snow was barely an inch thick, making traveling faster. They were already in sight of the forest.

Patting Canyon, Annie said, "I think we should stop here in the woods. It's cold and we all need a rest."

The cougar gave a grunt. "Very well. I have a feeling that we're being watched, though, and I'm not comfortable."

Tori just sat staring into space. She didn't seem like her old self. Lone One sidestepped nervously after hearing the cougar's premonition. It was lightly snowing and there was no wind for a change. The woods loomed ominously dark, even in daylight. Without much talk, the group made camp and ate some cold jerky and the preserved apples. As they fell asleep, a cold wind started to blow.

Golden Eagle was the fastest flyer in his kingdom, and the sun made his golden feathers gleam as if they had been painted with varnish. He led the way to Mount Frost. It soon became so cold that they had to fly lower to the ground, skimming the lakes and the treetops. It took people riding horses one to two days to walk this trail, but with a wingspan twice as long as a full grown horse, it took the eagles a few minutes. The huge birds split up as the trail thinned and the forest ended. Two followed, while the others went to recruit wolves.

Golden Eagle made a steep turn and landed lightly on the cold snow, flinching at the wetness. The others fell back in surprise when a cougar with a sandy gold pelt jumped out of the bushes.

"What do you want, *bird*?"

"Canyon, what is it?" A girl with brown hair and blue eyes walked out of their hideout holding one arm against her body.

"Eagles!" she cried in delight. Annie stared at them in delight wondering what golden eagles would be doing in this frozen wasteland.

The eagle in the front lifted his proud white head. "We have come as a favor to Red Mare to ask you to come back to Arfag immediately. She says the fate of the world is at stake."

Anger and relief hit Annie at the same time. She was mad at her 'friend' for deserting her, but glad she was safe.

"Why would *she* want *my* help after she deserted me? She betrayed me! That lying horse said 'We will rescue your sister, *we'll* save her!' Well, do you see Louise with me right now? Red left me after I entered the Toblin lair. Now she wants me to help her?"

Ashe eagle looked calmly at her; Annie felt embarrassed from saying too much and stepped back.

"Does that matter now?" he asked the girl. "That was the *past*, not the *now* or the *future*. She had a reason to leave. You escaped and you are fine. You have an ally, and now you have a chance to save the mare. You have to do this or risk never returning home and never seeing your sister or parents again. If we do nothing, no horses will be left alive. Do you *want* that to happen? Do you?"

Annie looked down to her feet and felt guilty. She could feel everyone looking at her, "No."

"What? I can't hear you," the eagle snapped.

Annie knew the bird really could hear her; he just wanted her to say it louder.

Anger and frustration burned in her.

"NO!" she screamed in the bird's face.

It looked calmly at her and said, "That's better. Use that anger bottled up in you to fight for the world, not to fight against Red Mare."

Annie sat down in the snow, not caring if it was cold or wet. She thought about Red, her noble head and her beautiful mane and tail, her powerful legs and graceful and commanding presence. *Could it really be that she was* forced *to go? That she had no choice? If so, why didn't she tell me?*

"Why didn't she tell me she was going to leave? Why did *she* keep that bottled up inside her like my anger?"

"Maybe she didn't want you to lose confidence, or she didn't want you to worry about her," the eagle replied.

Then Canyon spoke, "And why are YOU here? I'm sure you didn't fly all the way from Talon Peak just to help Annie with her anger problems."

Annie was close enough to smell the cougar's wild scent; she could smell wet leaves, prey, dirt, snow, and the smell of *wildness*. She could feel his power.

The eagle gazed at the mountain lion, unmoved by her sharp remark. "I've told you already, we've come to take you to Arfag to join us in the fight for world peace and freedom."

Canyon snarled and took a step closer.

"Friends, come on! Don't start a fight." Tori finally spoke up, clearly annoyed. "If there is going to be a war to save horses and freedom, then the *last* thing we need to do is spill blood over a minor argument."

The bird narrowed his eyes. "We must go now."

"How do you expect us to ride and run all the way to Arfag on foot and paw?" Canyon snapped.

"We don't; we'll carry you," the eagle replied.

"*What?*" they all asked in unison.

"Even Lone One and Canyon?"

"Oh, no, they'll have to walk," one of the birds snapped sarcastically. "Of course we'll carry them too."

"No filthy bird is going to but its talons on me!" Canyon hissed.

"Canyon," Annie tried to reason, "don't you want to help us?"

"Of course I do, but I don't want to ride on a filthy bird. I'll run."

"What do you mean? You can't get there in a few hours! You just said so yourself," Annie retorted.

"With no one on my back I can," Canyon replied. "When pushed, mountain lions are the fastest animals in the world! I'll show up. You can count on it."

"We don't have time to argue," the lead eagle said. "We'll just have to trust her. Let's go."

Tori took an old sweater and placed it over Lone One's head to keep him calm. A female eagle silently glided over and wrapped her talons gently around the horse's sides. Lone One started to spook and buck, but Tori spoke calmly to her, trying to settle her down. She finally did.

The lead bird looked at Annie and said, "You'd better ride with me." Annie nodded and grabbed a small blanket; it was the only thing left of her belongings, other then the books. As she stood next to the bird's side, he held out a wing. "Climb up onto my wing; gently please."

Crawling up on his wing, Annie straddled him like a horse. He was just wide enough for her to spread her legs out a little, but she had a hard time getting balanced. He shifted his weight and started to flap his wings. Tori climbed onto the same female that held her horse. With a nod to each other, the birds lifted into the air.

Being on a bird in the air was probably the most free she had ever felt in her life. Annie clung to the eagle's back as they lifted off into the air, squeezing around him with her arms and legs. They started to go faster as he climbed higher. Looking behind her, she saw Louise riding with her arms splayed out from her sides like she was flying all by herself. Annie tried to copy her sister, but fell forward. With a gasp, she imagined herself falling from the high altitude.

Tori looked relaxed, talking to her horse and her eagle like they had flown together for years. Her cape flapped behind her, the robin snug in her hood.

It started to get colder the higher they went, so they were relieved when the birds began their descent. Below they saw familiar landmarks. Soon they would be in Arfag.

———

Red galloped faster than she could ever imagine herself doing. *It's weird*, she thought. *I can run faster now than I could when I had my powers. So, what's happening? Did something go wrong? Do I still have my powers?*

Golden Feather flew next to her. They were now in sight of the town. They weren't tired, but felt empowered by a strong urgency that came from their hearts and minds. The eagle flew slowly and steadily, the sun gleaming on his feathers. His eyes burned with a fierce fire.

Golden Feather flew up ahead to tell the people of Arfag to clear the road but to remain present. He zoomed into the town, flying above the dazed crowd that lined the sides of the road. Then Red charged in. As she reached the middle of the town, she slid to a sudden halt. Everyone looked at her, but none approached. Then Red saw it; the people had blank, lifeless looks. The Cougar's shadow army had done their job. They rooted the free will out of the people so that they couldn't stop him.

"No," Red moaned in her soul.

"Yes," The blackness sneered.

Shadowy shapes spiraled out of the people's mouths. *"Nothing can stop us now, Red Mare. You are trapped and under our control."*

Golden Feather fell to the ground after giving an alarmed shriek. Red looked up and saw black bird shapes flying in circles around them.

"You're ours now, hay bag. No one can help you." The bird shapes surrounded the mare, swirling like a fog of despair and evil. She kicked out at them, but they kept coming. Slowly and menacing-

ly they advanced, snarling and growling. She didn't know what to do. Her powers were gone and she was just a regular horse. Wasn't she? Red tried her best not to let the shapes grab her, but they were closing in, and there was a thick pack of them.

Suddenly the shapes drew back, their eyes wide with fear. Blurs of golden shapes swarmed into them and they vanished. Behind her, Red felt a familiar presence. A feeling overcame her, filled with sorrow and joy, relief and stress. *Annie.*

"Red!"

Annie jumped off the bird as quickly as she could and, despite her anger, she ran to the horse. Annie sensed Red was different. It was like a part of her was missing. *Was it her joy?*

"Red, what happened to you?"

Annie stopped short of hugging her neck. The horse looked at her, and sadness filled her once joyful eyes.

"Annie, I don't know how to make you understand, but I hope you will *try*. I don't have my powers anymore; they were taken away from me. That's why I left—because I was *forced* to. I would never have abandoned you on purpose. Please believe me."

The girl stood silent, for she couldn't find any words to say. The mare stood there, too, powerless. Then Annie rushed to her with tears in her eyes. A girl reunited with her horse! Annie wrapped her arms around the familiar neck, breathing in her comforting earthy scent. She caressed Red's reed-like mane.

"Why didn't you tell me? I wouldn't have been mad at you. I would have understood."

"Some things are better left unsaid until they happen. Do you know why you're here?"

"To help save your world, like the prophecy foretold."

"Annie?" Louise was standing behind them. She was curious about her sister's relationship with a beautiful red horse.

"Louise, come over here. I'd like you to meet someone," Annie invited.

Her sister ran over with childlike enthusiasm.

"Louise, this is my dear friend Red Mare. She helped me rescue you, but had to leave before you could meet her."

"She's beautiful!"

"Thank you," Red replied.

Her sister jumped back in surprise. "You, you can talk?"

"Yes, in this world, I can talk."

"Wow, talking horses! Are you fast?"

"Very," Red said proudly.

Annie noticed her sister was already becoming attached to the 'magical' mare. She mounted Red, who still carried her saddle on her back after all this time.

"When do we expect the next attack?"

"Tonight, the night of no moon."

"That's why I've been having those dreams! Are we fighting a large, shadowy cougar by any chance?"

Red looked surprised. "Yes. How did you know?"

"I had a dream, it was so real. I was in a cave and heard a cougar talk to his minions about a battle; but then he saw me. He somehow knew that you left me and he tried to get me to use my anger to destroy you. Why would he want to do that?"

"He's an enemy of the horse-world and full of evil, hate and spitefulness."

"Annie, can I ride with you too?" Louise asked hopefully.

"Not now, little girl," Red nudged her happily. "Your sister and I have more work to do. Maybe later."

Annie wrapped her fingers through her beloved Red's smooth, glistening mane. It had always been there when she needed something to hold onto. "Let's do what we must," she said.

Red reared and cantered back into the center of the town.

———

People were rubbing their sleepy eyes, looking dazed and confused.

"What happened?" Annie asked.

"The shadow army has been controlling them," said a familiar man.

"We just chased the rest away, and now the people are coming out of their trance."

The man approached them. He was slightly rounder than before, and now wore a nice suit. His broad face held a wide smile and his arms were outstretched.

"My friends! You've come to help us?" It was the innkeeper, Mr. Beeter.

"Mr. Beeter!" Annie exclaimed excitedly, smiling from ear to ear.

"Hello, Amy, how are you? What are you doing back here?"

"We're here to warn you of a coming danger, one that holds the fate of horses and freedom alike." Red answered for her with a serious snort.

"Oh dear! You'll need an army, won't you? Townspeople are not much of an army," Mr. Beeter replied worriedly. "We've been trying to fight the evil ones for months. They always come back."

"We have the great birds of Talon Peak and the wolves of Mt. Frost to help us. We have Annie, Tori, Louise and myself. You have plenty of farmers who own horses and a blacksmith who can make us weapons. That's all we have, but that will have to be enough."

"No, you're wrong about that."

Red jumped at the deep voice coming from behind them. Annie twisted around in her saddle to look also. There stood a tall man with a long black beard, wearing a tattered grey and brown robe. He looked older than most of the farmers in the area, with his long grey hair down past his shoulders. He had a proud and an almost magical appearance. There was a faint glow around him.

"Who are you?" Annie asked in amazement. She was thrown off balance as Red bent her head low, like she was bowing.

The man chuckled, "Now, now Red Mare. No immortal horse need bow before me."

What is going on here? Annie wondered.

"I'm a mortal horse now, your Grace," Red replied.

"No, your power has never left you. That's why you haven't felt it return to you." the wizard replied.

"Okay, what is going on here?" Annie asked in annoyance. It seemed like the two had completely forgotten she was there.

"Annie, our dear Annie. So, we finally meet!" the ghostly man greeted.

"Who are you?"

"I'm a wizard."

"Does that mean you know magic?" Annie replied hopefully.

"Yes, and I've been working on something you'll all be glad to see. It will be useful when we fight the shadow army. Tell Mr. Beeter to prepare the townsfolk for the upcoming war."

The innkeeper had been standing listening anyway, so he nodded and walked off hurriedly.

Just then Tori came galloping over. "Daddy!" she cried, "Dad!"

"Child! Tori!" He calmly walked up to the galloping Lone One, stopping her with a wave of his pinky finger.

"Tori, come here child." her father said with outstretched arms.

The teen jumped off her horse and into his arms with the joy of a small child. He rubbed her shoulders and whispered in her ear. After one last hug, they parted and Tori mounted her horse again, her eyes filled with determination. The wizard looked up at her, smiled at her with affection, and patted her leg. He then waved his hand for all to follow. As they walked through the grassy fields of Arfag, they could hear Mr. Beeter up ahead gathering the people and calling out warnings.

The inside of the hut was very warm. A fireplace burned with a controlled ferocity that warmed the room in seconds. Annie watched the wizard's beard turn a silvery white when he took out a small dagger, which itself glowed with a blue light. Lone One was in the stable, but Red had the privilege to come into the hut because of her status. The wizard took the dagger and slowly walked toward the fire. He pointed it out like he was going to fight someone; then he slowly pushed it into the flames. It turned blue, then white, and suddenly—a small swirl of light came out of the fire.

They all watched closely as Tori handed her father a piece of metal. Muttering a few words, the wizard threw it into the fire. A flash of light blinded them for a second. Annie gasped as Tori's father reached into the flames with his bare hand! She waited for agonizing screams from burning flesh, but not a sound came from his stern mouth.

"Now watch! The fire has created the one temperature where magic can be used without hazards. Now this one piece of metal will become ten shields and fifteen swords!" The wizard removed his hand from the flame, muttering words and phrases they couldn't understand. Soon, shapes bathed in light settled onto the floor of the cabin. As the wizard removed the knife, the fire returned to red, orange and yellow.

"Wow! Look at those!" Annie exclaimed.

Admiring his work, he turned to Annie and said, "Ah, these are not just any old swords and shields, but *magic* swords and shields. They are crafted in light, magic, and fire—the three enemies of darkness. They are the strongest weapons we have against them."

"How did the eagles kill them so quickly?" Annie asked, remembering the shadows vanishing as soon as they made contact with them.

"Great. Wonderful question!" the wizard exclaimed, sitting down into an old rocking chair that creaked as it moved. "Eagles and birds fly in the daylight, and golden eagles especially resemble light. Fire, magic, and wind are things that shadows fear most. When you give light, darkness disappears. When you light a candle, it is not as dark as it was. When you use magic, you use light. Where there is light, there can be no darkness."

"If these weapons are so powerful, why don't you make enough for the whole town?" she said.

His enthusiastic smile vanished a little. "My magic only goes so far, my dear. This power will suck the energy from you. That's the one price you pay for magic. It drains you of your life force."

"What about our other problem?" Red asked.

"What's that?" the wizard said, raising his bushy eyebrows.

"The fact that we have five hours to find enough fighters."

"Are there any more wizards that could help us?" Annie asked hopefully.

"No, there can only be two of us on this planet at once. One practices the dark arts, and I practice the white arts. The other wizard would sooner lose his magic and die than help us."

"Too bad the Kingdom had to fall so many years ago. The royal guard was well trained and disciplined. We wouldn't have had to worry about not having enough *trained* creatures to help." Red said.

"Why did it fall?" Annie asked.

"The royal family was murdered by the Toblins, and their knights scattered over the land in hiding," Red replied. "That was many years ago, and the generation lines have probably died out by now."

"Not quite." The wizard looked her over. He closed his eyes for a second before saying, "In this room we have a royal blood relative. Someone in our midst is the true queen of our world."

Chapter 12

Sitting in a dark room that lay in shambles, a figure yawned. She had been sitting for hours among the rubble of her demolished room. The tapestries were torn and the windows were shattered. Her bed and handmade wooden dresser lay in splinters. She stood up and brushed the dirt and dust from her dress and walked out. The southern wall of the palace lay in ruin. The royal guard had scattered and left years ago, leaving the royal family behind.

"Why can't they just let me go out into the world and ask for help? We can't always take care of ourselves." She said out loud to no one.

The hallway was mostly intact except for a few shattered vases and torn tapestries. She was the princess, twelve years of age. Her red hair was not common in her family, so she stood out from the beginning. Her mother and father demanded that she stay hidden, so nobody would know that they exist and are defenseless. She disagreed entirely. The royal family needed help, and she was determined to find it.

The princess ran along the corridors silently, slipping through a couple of rooms where a few people sat whispering. She opened a door and slipped outside. After the castle collapsed, few horses survived. Those who didn't die were stolen. A few of them escaped, however, and returned unharmed.

Entering the stable, she looked at the stalls. Four horse heads came to the front of their enclosures and snorted a greeting. Walking to the armory in search of weapons and tack, she came across the royal cart. On the front was a picture of four rearing horses, each a different color.

After dragging out the cart, she went back and grabbed four harnesses, taking care that they didn't get tangled. She hung three of them on an empty bridle holder and took the fourth into the first stall. She patted the golden cream mare on her smooth pink nose and the mare nickered back. The princess slipped the neckpiece over the horse's head and snapped everything together. Going to the black stallion next, she led him over and clipped his harness to the wagon. She then hooked the brown mare next to him. Last, but not least, she hooked up a beautiful fiery-red stallion.

The princess then went into the armory and grabbed four blue army cloths to slip over the horses' heads. They looked like they were charging into battle, with their blankets flowing down to their knees! She then grabbed a flag and placed it on the cart before pushing the door open with a bang. She ran to the wagon, grabbing reins in one hand, the flag in the other.

Clucking with her tongue she yelled, "Yah, Flame, yah, Star!"

The four horses charged forward at a very fast trot, pulling the cart with ease. They headed toward the one town that had been ruled by her family many years ago—the town of Arfag.

Annie was stunned. *Is it me? My sister? Her parents didn't have anything to do with this world, did they?* The wizard turned on his heel and strode over to the window. Red shook her mane and pawed the ground.

"Red, is that true?" Annie asked, bewildered.

"Yes," she replied.

"Then Louise is the rightful ruler of this land?"

"No. You are." Red said.

Annie felt stunned and speechless.

"Are you sure no one is left of the royal family?" Red asked the wizard. "What if the family lives and they are in hiding? What would we do then?"

"If there are any members of the royal family left, they must step down for the sake of this world," the wizard proclaimed.

"We have company," Tori said, standing up abruptly and looking into the distance. Annie saw that she wiped away tears as she spoke.

"Tori?" Annie asked, "What's wrong? Where is Heart's Song?"

Tori's eyes were full of grief. "He's dead. I buried him while you were talking to the innkeeper. I can still hear his song in my heart."

"Oh, Tori! I'm so sorry. He was your friend and such a good bird." Annie put her arm around her friend as they looked out the window together. On the horizon, and just over the hills, was the shape of a horse-drawn cart approaching.

"Let's go greet her," the wizard said, striding out the door.

"How does he know?" Annie began to ask.

The teen stopped her. "He's a wizard. He can see far better with his mind than we can with our eyes."

The girls mounted their horses and followed the wizard. He seemed to glide over the grass. As they got closer to the cart, Annie could see that it was indeed driven by a girl holding a flag. There were four horses pulling it.

"Why is she carrying a flag, and why do the horses have blue blankets over them?" Annie asked.

Red asked, "Does she have red hair?"

"Yes, she does," the wizard called excitedly over his shoulder.

Red picked up speed and went into a gallop. She wanted to meet the princess before anybody else.

As they got close enough to see her clearly, Annie raised her hand in greeting. The mare slowed to a trot as the red haired teenager slowed her horses to a stop.

"Greetings," Annie called out.

As they approached the cart the stranger nervously raised her hand in greeting. "I'm Windrider, the princess of this land."

Red bowed in greeting. "My dear Princess Windrider, you have been away so long! The last time I saw you, you were a baby! We thought the royal family had been killed, or had deserted us. Because of your absence, a new line of royal blood had to be chosen."

"What nonsense!" she exclaimed in a sharp tone. "I'm the *real princess*. No one has the right to take away my throne. Wait a minute. You're a-a talking horse!"

Annie instinctively drew her sword.

"Calm down, Annie," said Red. "Let me handle this."

"Yes, and your horses can talk, too," Red told the princess. "But they have been silenced in order not to give your location away. Ask your father. Their voices were a danger to your lives."

"No creature should be silenced for a human's life. She looked at her own horses and said, "I command you to speak!"

The horses whinnied and nickered. Finally, the fiery red stallion pranced forward. "Red Mare, thank you for coming and giving our voices back again!"

The golden mare shook her head and gave a melodious sigh of delight before saying, "Yes, thank you!"

The brown mare and black stallion both reluctantly grunted thanks, too.

Red reared and cut the harnesses with her sharp hooves as she came down. "You are free now, royal horses. That means you have free will. Choose to serve the new royal family, serve Windrider, or run free."

The red stallion walked up to Red. "I choose to serve you and the new royal family." The brown mare and black stallion joined him beside Red, but the golden mare did not. Instead, she stood by Windrider and nudged her arm. "Red Mare, I thank you for releasing our gift of tongue, but I've pledged my loyalty to the Princess Windrider. It would be a dishonor for me to break that pledge."

"Very well, a pledge is a thing we must keep and hold true to our hearts. Horses should never break a pledge they have made to a human."

Windrider mounted her loyal mare and said, "Tell me, what is this talk about a war?"

"The shadow warriors are planning an attack. They are going to try to take over our world. We hope to recruit forces to join us in our fight against them."

Three of the four royal horses neighed in fear and pranced around Red, as if hoping she would protect them. The auburn stallion stood by Red's side.

"Red Mare, I will gladly fight with you."

"Do you have a name?"

"Flame," he said, as the wind swept through his fiery red mane.

"Are you fast?" Red inquired.

"Faster than most," he whinnied proudly. "Who else will fight with us?"

"Villagers, a wizard, a bunch of horses, wolves, birds, two girls and a royal pain. Do any of you know of anyone else who can help?" Red asked.

"I know the dragons and the coyotes would if they didn't live on the other side of the world," the wizard joined in.

Suddenly, Annie remembered her new friend. "Canyon! Canyon has yet to arrive."

"I doubt just *one* cougar will be much help," Red said with a sigh.

The sun was high in the sky, causing them to look at one another nervously. "We don't have much time," Red said, glancing at Windrider. "I need you to go back to the castle and get anyone with a willing heart who can carry a sword. Bring them here as fast as you can."

"I'll let no horse order me around! I choose to do this on my own accord," the princess said with a huff. She set off for the castle.

Red muttered as she watched her leave. "What a royal pain! 'No horse can order me around because I am a princess,' Red mimicked. "Why didn't she return years ago, instead of hiding with her family like scared rabbits? If her family had shown some bravery, maybe this all could have been prevented!"

"The past is the past," said the wizard.

" Let's go back to Arfag and get the town ready," Annie suggested, trying to change the subject.

Flame whinnied and called the brown mare and stallion. Tori and her dad galloped over on Lone One. They all headed back to town and marveled when they saw that most of the townspeople were already wearing some sort of armor or holding a shield and weapon.

Red shouted out, "People of Arfag!" Everyone turned to listen as the mare continued. "We face a threat that lives in the pit of darkness. They controlled you for the last month and now it is time to fight back! For your freedom, for your beloved horses, you must stand up and join us in taking back the land!"

A cheer rose up from the farmers and shopkeepers.

Mr. Beeter started to yell, "Horses! Freedom! World! Horses! Freedom! World!"

Soon all the people joined in the chant, raising their weapons into the air as they shouted "Horses! Freedom! World!

Annie was so proud that so many people were willing to fight. *But would they be alive in the next few hours? Would they prevail and defeat the shadow army? Is this what it feels like to head into battle,* she wondered—*to worry about the lives of people you didn't even know you cared about? To worry you won't do your best or let your friends down? What if my sister gets hurt? What would she do if I were killed? This is a horrifying day. I wonder where Louise is right now?*

It was then she realized Louise was missing!

———

"You're sure you didn't see her leave?" Annie asked frantically.

Mr. Beeter rubbed the smooth spot on the back of his head. "No, Miss Amy! I do remember seeing her talk to the brown mare, though. I could tell they liked each other, but I've never heard of a horse running off with a child. They were looking at a map, but I didn't pay much heed."

"Do you think…?" Annie turned to Red, "Do you think she went to find more people to help us?"

"I don't know," Red said. "The royal horses are experts at keeping hidden, and that brown mare was no exception. She would be impossible to track, but I'm sure she would protect your sister with her life."

"Louise is a smart little girl on a noble horse. Things will work out for her," the innkeeper said, trying to cheer Annie. "My friends are making snacks for the townspeople to boost their energy as they prepare for battle. The horses are being fed our best grain and hay. They will have a little time to relax before their warm-up. Everyone here has at least one horse, and all can fight with their hands and ride with their legs."

"The shadow army will figure out quickly that we are helpless without our horses. They'll fight them first and then, when all the horses are killed or chased away, they'll go for us." Annie argued.

"Good point," Mr. Beeter said, "I'll get on that right away." The man ran out of the inn and started talking to people in the street, arranging practice drills without their horses.

———•———

Galloping over the bushes and gliding over logs, Louise felt much like her sister had when she first started her adventure. Now it was her turn to save her sister, her sister's friends, and the whole world! Provided she could get to *them* in time! Her brown mare was strong, fast, and had a mysterious perspective on life. She didn't like to talk much, but she was able to send telepathic waves into Louise's mind.

Louise hated her name. "What kind of a name is Louise, anyway?" she mumbled to herself. She also hated the fact that everybody tried to baby her just because she was five! "I'll be six in a few days," she muttered, "and then I'll show everybody how brave and heroic I can be. They'll never baby me again. I'll be just like Annie."

"Are you sure we're going the right way?" the mare silently asked in her mind.

The young girl's fantasy vanished from her mind's eye and she was brought back to the present. "Sure, I'm sure. The map said to head toward the Weeping Swamp then take a sharp turn to the right before you hit the water."

"Okay, but can you focus on riding? *Please*? You're sitting too far back on my back!"

"Sorry," Louise said, sitting up straight and moving forward.

They veered to the right and struggled through thick vines while dodging rocks and logs along the trail. *This is insane!* Louise thought.

"I know," replied the mare in her mind.

"I'm still not comfortable with you reading my thoughts."

"I don't 'read' your thoughts, I scan them. Only when I want to answer do I read your thoughts. Get it?"

"Nope," said Louise aloud.

The gallop turned into a fast walk as they dodged vines, trees, rocks, and logs.

"How could this place be on a map? I don't see a trail," the mare asked, feeling frustrated, cut and sore.

"This has to be the way through because all the wha … !"

"Louise?" The mare whipped around and the girl was no longer on her back.

"I'm up here. I think a vine grabbed hold of me and dragged me upwards."

"How can a vine drag upwards? It can tangle but it can't drag!"

"Please help me down, said the girl. I think the map tricked us...."

"Why?"

"Because we're in the thicket filled with vines that think!"

"I've heard of vines that kill; they wrap themselves around creatures, like an anaconda. You think these vines think?"

"Please get me down from here!" She started to struggle, and the vines became tighter with each movement.

"I'm lacking in height. You'll have to figure out a way to get yourself down," the horse said.

Louise unwrapped one arm and then another, but as she tried to unwrap her legs, the vines started moving around her again, tighter and tighter.

"Help me!"

"Don't-ddddon't panic. DON'T PANIC!" The horse reared and ripped the lower vines in half with her sharp hooves. They writhed and squirmed like animals in pain. Louise tried to loosen the remaining vines but they pulled themselves taut, squeezing her again with such force it would've fractured her arms with a tiny more pressure.

"Ahhhhhhhhhh!" Burning pain shot through her arm. The vines continued wrapping around her until only her face showed.

"Vine beings of the swamp!" she yelled, short of breath.

The mare looked up at the girl. *What is she trying to do?*

"My friend and I are only passing through your domain to find the Great Kingdom of the Leopards. We need help with a battle that is close at hand. If you kill me, thousands will have no hope to live after the world has been conquered. I ask you to let us go. Please!"

Silence followed for a few heartbeats.

"You have already entered the Kingdom of the Leopards. What would a human like you want with us?" A voice called out with a booming voice, "Vines! Let her go."

The vines loosened and Louise fell to the ground. The mare rushed to her side. There standing in a ray of light, was a golden leopard.

The sun was setting and the war would soon begin. A few stars were making an appearance, but there was no moon on the horizon. Birds of all shapes and sizes flew in circles above. Their job was to give a signal when they spotted the advancing army. Most of the people held torches lit with bright orange flames.

Annie sat on Red's back and tried to stay calm by concentrating on her breathing. Flame stood next to them; her silver leg, head, and neck armor reflected red from the fires and the sunset.

Red wore a nice lightweight saddle that was easy to maneuver in yet strong enough not to be punctured by swords. They stood on a hill looking down onto the meadow that would soon become a battlefield. It was strangely quiet and empty. Thoughts of what might happen surrounded every person like a fog. The air was stagnant; it smelled of sweat and fear.

Annie couldn't help but feel that this war was senseless. She wondered if more people would survive if they just surrendered right at the start. But then again, if they surrendered, they'd all be killed anyway. She wanted to go home and crawl in bed and read a book to Louise. She wanted to leave the fighting to someone else while she sat safely on the sidelines. She knew that was not possible, but fear kept nagging at her heart. *Breathe!* She told herself. *Breathe!*

"Red?"

"Are you frightened, Annie?"

"Yes, I'm scared that I am leading us into a war we cannot win!"

"The odds may be against us, Annie, but we have more to lose than they do. Isn't that what powers the fight to greatness?" Her voice increased in volume as she continued. "When we're all dead and gone, the little children will ask their parents to tell them the story of the great battle when good triumphed over evil. It will inspire them to do what's right, even when the odds are against *them*. This battle will be remembered in history."

Apparently Red spoke loud enough for the whole army to hear and they cheered and clapped and raised their weapons in the air.

A rumbling like an earthquake shook the ground and horses and people alike struggled to remain on their feet. The King of the Golden Eagles flew to the front of the army calling out "The shadow army has breached land!"

Murmurs of fear arose from the crowd. The wolf leader stood behind Red and Flame, and the eagles flew around them. They all began to sing, and soon the mournful sound was like a battle cry. Everyone—the eagles and birds, the horses and humans—chanted as one. "Horses, Freedom, World!"

In the distance, a cloud of black rose into the sky and it spread across the heavens toward them. Creatures from the woods joined ranks instead of hiding; they too could sense something important was beginning. A pack of feral dogs and cats stood together, with their claws at the ready. Squirrels joined together to throw nuts and small rocks. Mice stood ready to trip and bite.

"If things get bad, retreat to the castle. It will give you more protection!" Red screeched and reared.

"Hey, hey you," a voice called.

Annie twisted in her seat and saw Windrider galloping to them with a group of fifteen armed men. The princess took her place at the front with the leaders.

"I thought you didn't have anymore horses?" Red asked curiously.

"I managed to find a few of the old royal guard in the farms nearby. They were willing to come out of hiding and join the fight."

Red nodded to them and they nodded in return. "Well done, Windrider," she said.

The shadow was getting closer now, and the horses pranced nervously. Annie tried to take more deep breaths, but they turned shallow and fast. It made her feel faint.

Red glanced back at her and said, "We're with each other to the end."

"To the end."

"To the end," the wolf leader, Flame, and the Eagle King said together.

As the cloud of shadows reached the field, shapes started to form. Dragons and monsters appeared, as well as wolves, horses, people and coyotes. The tactic was ingenious. It would be harder now to tell enemy from friend. They charged through the field and Annie raised her sword. The army cheered as they charged down the hill.

———

Farther away, other shapes flew across the ground. Tan, golden, brown and black—they raced along, an urgency powering them.

"Come on, the battle is starting!" The lead shape called. "The sun is setting! We have to hurry!"

The shapes raced even faster, their paws almost invisible. The leader urged them onward, racing through the forest covered with thorns. They were like comets of sand and dust speeding across the land. "Hurry, they're counting on us!"

———

Annie and Red led the charge with Flame, the eagle and the wolf along side them. Windrider and her small army galloped close behind. They continued to chant as they raced down the slope, pointing their weapons forward. No thoughts raced through Annie's head as the first shadow figure threw itself at her. The eagle intercepted and slashed it to the ground. It shrieked as the two armies crashed together.

Annie looked around and noted they were outnumbered by

two thousand at least. The creatures kept changing shapes to intimidate their enemies, and it was working. One moment the wolves were fighting a horse—next a dragon. Red slashed one of the dragons down; managing to dodge the fireball it blew at her just in time. The wolves then jumped on the dragon's unguarded belly, and it vanished within heartbeats.

It was overwhelming—as one creature advanced on one side; five others would advance on the other. Annie slashed her glowing sword at a shadow cougar as it screeched and lunged at her. She made a deep gash in its shoulder, but its claws were in Red's mane. Annie screamed and tried to push the thing off, but it wouldn't budge. Red reared and suddenly, the creature was caught in the talons of a swooping eagle, where it met its death.

Flame galloped toward them, kicking off a creature as he did.

"Red! The Eagle King is down! We must help him!"

They raced to the area where black dragons raged. The birds swarmed around their heads, trying to hold the creatures back as they jabbed at their eyes with their talons. Annie saw one large golden eagle on the ground with a bloody wing. He hopped around, slashing at shadows. She saw that he was tiring and wouldn't be able to hold out much longer. Just then a dragon charged, breathing black fire, its eyes blazing with the color of blood.

Annie raised her sword and told Red, "The stomach, get me to the stomach."

Red snorted and dodged one way and then the other, much like a cat trying to catch two bugs at once. Annie aimed for the dragon's middle as the creature opened its wings and spit fire around them. Encircled by a ring of flames, Annie yelled into Red's ear, "You'll have to jump!"

"Be ready!" Red yelled back.

Red scanned the monster's movements above them as Annie lifted her sword. She felt the mare tense before bursting into a canter and jumping over the black flames. With a well-placed thrust of her sword, the girl sliced at the dragon's stomach. Dodging just in time, it only sustained a scratch. It dove at them again and Red jumped once more, giving Annie another chance to kill it. The timing was perfect. The girl saw her chance and she took a breath. It was now or never. Annie stood up in the saddle and jumped into the air.

———

Red turned around. Annie wasn't on her back. The dragon lay dead on the ground and was slowly vanishing, its rancid smell mixed with the sharp odor of pine. Blood was everywhere. Red found herself wishing that her sense of smell were less developed.

Where did she go? She didn't see the girl anywhere. Fearing the worst, the mare felt a horrific anger and an overwhelming need for revenge. When the people saw that Red was fighting without Annie, they too thought the girl was dead. It made them all fight a little harder in their grief and anger.

Red stomped creatures to the ground and smashed them to dust. Flame was shocked to see that Red was glowing! The light of the Healer and the light of Joy had returned. Her powers were back! Red crushed the shadows and Flame fought tirelessly by her side, as more and more shadow warriors disappeared beneath their hooves.

Then, a loud screech turned every eye toward the hill. The last rays of the setting sun illuminated brown and sandy-colored hides.

"Look, Flame!" Red shouted. "The cougars have come! Canyon has brought a whole pack of fighters!"

———

The hoof beats thundered in her ears and the spicy smell of wild vines tickled her nose. The flowers glittered pink in the last rays of the sun, and the water from a stream smelled delicious. *If only they could stop and drink*! Louise urged them onward. Hopefully they would make it to the battle before the sun went down completely.

The cougars ran roaring down the hill, tackling the shadows with earsplitting screeches. Windrider pranced on Star below, going in circles trying to calm her frightened horse. She noticed a shadow creature stealthily crawl behind a boulder sticking out of the ground. Below it was a deep ditch. The creature looked like it was stalking something. *A child could be in there!*

Galloping over, the princess dismounted quietly and climbed onto the big rock; the creature didn't see her because it was too intent on its prey. Windrider saw the faint shape of a girl lying on her back. In one hand the girl held a glowing white sword. She had brown hair, the color of oak trees in autumn. Her arms and head were bloody, but she was breathing.

"Annie ..." she whispered under her breath.

Drawing her sword, Windrider jumped down in front of the unconscious girl as the creature had yet to turn the corner. The rocks below her were rounded and had large cracks, as if the rocks themselves had fought and gotten scars. The princess heard the girl whimper.

"Windrider?" the weak voice asked.

The shape pounced, turning into a cougar. It hissed. The cat and princess flung themselves at each other, and Annie watched helplessly as the cougar transformed itself into a sword-fighting human. A knife went flying by her head and pierced her arm. She screamed in pain. Windrider turned and swiftly pulled out the knife with her free hand.

"Put some pressure on it!" she yelled to Annie as the shadow raised his sword.

"Look out!" screeched the girl.

The princess twisted around, but not in time. The sword plunged through her heart and she fell to her knees, then onto her back. Dead.

"Windrider!"

The shadow laughed and turned into the same dragon she had fought when they left the Sea Unicorn—the same one who had hypnotized her and made her stab Tori in the heart!

"Thought you got rid of me, didn't you?" it leered.

Annie looked at the princess lying dead on the rocks and reached for the sword resting at her side. Her left arm was bloody and limp. *Act like you're helpless,* she thought to herself. *The shock of it being destroyed will be more satisfying then!*

"Please, don't hurt me," she called weakly.

"Hurt you? Why would I want to hurt you? I want to *kill* you!" It seemed to glide up to her, its eyes turning red, the stench of death filling the air.

Annie gripped her sword with her right hand and clenched her jaw. "I said, don't mess with me!"

It lunged and she threw. The dragon fell back and hit the sharp rocks below, the hilt of the glowing sword resting in its chest. Annie didn't feel sorry for it at all as she watched it dissolve.

She stumbled down the cliff and crawled over to the creature before it vanished. When she yanked the sword from its body it made a gushy sound as it slid free. Annie tried to get to Windrider, but had a hard time climbing back up with one arm. It hurt so much! When she reached the princess's body, she wept. The princess was a brave fighter and died protecting her. Annie would always wonder what she did to deserve such a sacrifice.

Looking skyward, she saw it was getting dark and clouds were moving in. The dead feel of the air meant rain was coming. Crawling up slowly, she finally managed to get out of the ditch. She grabbed a boulder and painfully hoisted herself up.

She saw that Canyon had arrived—along with a whole pack of her followers. A rumbling and growling came from the forest behind her, and she dived under an overhang of the rock as a thousand shapes of leopards pounced over the crevice and into the battle. *How did they get here? Who brought them? Louise!*

Annie scrambled to the top and saw Red, Flame, and Louise fighting. Her heart broke when she heard her sister let out a loud wail. She looked for Canyon and saw that the cat was fighting furiously alongside a leopard and a wolf. The five shadows were losing.

"Canyon!" she called, "Canyon, over here!"

The lion looked up with her green eyes to see Annie waving a throbbing hand. "Annie!" Their eyes met and the cougar raced to her side. She gave a growl of delight and sniffed the girl.

"Look at you! You're surely beat up! I heard you were dead."

"The dragon hit me before I killed it. By all accounts I should be dead!"

"It surely is a miracle! Get on my back. We have the world to save!"

Annie struggled on. Her arm continued to throb and her head felt light and woozy. It was hard to concentrate but she tried her best to hold steady. Canyon waited for her to get settled before taking off—first at a walk, then a trot, then her jump-gallop-gait. Canyon sped toward Red and the others, her human passenger in danger of falling off. Annie was so tired she just wanted to lie down and sleep.

"Red! Louise! Flame!" Canyon screeched as Annie started to fall.

She couldn't hold on any longer. Her strength left her. *I'm so tired ... so thirsty ...* She tumbled off, unconscious.

There was darkness. Emptiness. Nothing. She knew she was lying somewhere, but she didn't know where. Her arms and legs were numb and felt like heavy stones. A familiar light appeared. The pink-white light and the sweet scent of flowers wrapped around her like a blanket. A red horse the color of the desert sun stood before her, in its mouth a glittering pink flower shaped like a star. The horse placed it gently onto the girl's cold hands resting on her chest. The horse reared and looked up at the sky. The moon was not shining, but the stars were plentiful and glittered eerily.

"Wake..." Red whispered like soft breeze.

"Wha ... !" Annie gasped and sat up.

Red, Louise, Flame and Canyon cheered as she opened her eyes.

"Now that you're awake, drink some water, but not too fast! If you can, get on my back," Red ordered. Annie pulled herself up with the help of her friends and drank a few sips of water. Louise looked so happy it seemed she had invented the smile. Annie shook her head as if to clear it from fog. She sat up straighter and noticed her arm was bandaged. She felt better.

Up ahead, three dragons dissolved into the air, thanks to the birds. The smaller shadows were being driven back by the wolves. Both armies lost great numbers, but it looked like the enemy was losing.

A rumbling shook the ground, and a great shape materialized out of the ground. It was the Cougar of Darkness. He raked the birds from the sky with his giant claws and set out to kill those who dared defy him. After a terrible few minutes, the only ones left standing or who had not run away were Annie, Red, Flame, Louise, Canyon and the wolf leader. He crouched forward with blood dripping from his fangs.

"I've warned you, he laughed. No one can defeat me! I can finish you off without hardly lifting a paw." Then with his claws unsheathed, he pounced at them. Everyone scattered in different directions. Annie watched in horror as he cornered the wolf. Red reared and raced to save him, but it was too late. A fateful bite was already made—the wolf leader was dead.

They all shouted in anger and threw themselves at the beast, no longer concerned about danger. The Cougar of Darkness hissed and batted each of them away like flies. Annie held on tight as Red reared again. They both started to glow with a white light. The light was warm and felt powerful and Annie closed her eyes as she relished its power rushing through them. Girl and horse became one. Moving as one, they galloped toward the creature, and Annie raised her sword.

Flame kicked the lion in the paw and darted off in the opposite direction as Red rushed by close enough for Annie to stab the beast in the hip. He screeched and whipped around, but Red Mare was still near enough for Annie to give another deep gash to his stomach. He fell onto his back and roared.

Jumping up, he shook away the pain and pounced again. Thunder exploded from the sky and the rain began to fall as an arrow flew through the air and into his snout. Annie turned and saw Tori standing next to her father on the hilltop. Lightning darted from cloud to cloud until one bolt found its target and hit the cougar. He screeched in agony and fell, blood gushing from his nose. Turning to Canyon, he snarled, "Traitor! How could you fight for *them?*"

Canyon lifted her head in defiance.

"I am no traitor. I've done what is right, and I'm not ashamed. I hate you. Cougars are not the evil beings you wanted them to be. You invaded our thoughts, and you made us do evil things."

"You are a traitor and a disgusting piece of trash!" spat the Cougar of Darkness. I gave you nine lives, and I'm going to take them back. You remember what happens when you've already used one, don't you?"

"Yes. You stole my heart."

Black clouds started to swarm around Canyon, but she defiantly raised her head to them. A dark light engulfed her, and she twitched like she was being shocked.

"Canyon!" Annie screamed, but the dark light vanished and the mountain lion fell dead.

"No!" Red and Annie cried together. The light around them grew brighter. The red mare reared and commanded, "I call upon the Four Hooves!"

The lightning continued to ricochet in the sky while thunder shook the ground. Red and Annie stood firm as the cougar stalked toward them, blood dripping from his fangs.

"My, my, look at you two. You think you can call upon the Four

Hooves to defeat me? You're not even one of them anymore Red Mare, remember?" Lightning lit the sky and another arrow hit Him in the paw but he pulled it out with his teeth.

"Little girl over there on the hilltop, I advise you to stop with the arrows—or face a terrible and certain death!"

"Threaten my friend again and you'll be dust!" Annie said defiantly.

"Brave words from one so little!" The cougar laughed at her in ridicule and came at them.

Red shifted under the girl and kept looking up at the night sky as if waiting. Lightning flared across the dark clouds and lit them up. Annie looked into the streaks and saw three shapes. They reared and galloped out of the night, gradually gaining color as they came closer. One was white, one was grey, and the other was bay. The horse shapes raced around the cougar, and then stood by Red's side.

"I thought Sunrise said that you weren't part of the group anymore," the grey stallion snorted.

"He did, but I guess some of my powers stayed with me," said Red. "I guess as long as I have power, I'm still part of you. And you are a part of me."

The horses all started to glow in different colors. The bay was a golden-white, the colt was a pure white light, and the grey stallion had a stormy-ash light. Red neighed a war cry and raised her front hooves into the air. The three did the same, and Annie held on tightly as they turned to face the Cougar.

He sat on his haunches with an exquisite beauty that all cats possessed, evil or good. Lightning struck the Cougar again and again, but he just shook it off like drops of rain. He stood again, to face the challenge before him.

The band of four horses stood menacingly in front of their enemy and pawed their hooves at the ground as the girl raised her sword. Lightning formed a ball above the cat's head and struck him again with a mighty force. He jerked in pain, but leapt off the ground in a fiery rage. Flames rose up His legs and around his head like a tornado. Annie watched as the fire formed a ball and went airborne.

"No!" Red charged, intent on stopping the blazing ball before it hit the wizard. It was too late. Tori screamed as her father fell backwards from the impact. He lay ablaze on the hilltop.

Rushing to his side, Tori rolled him along the ground to smother the flames. She then turned her fury toward the beast as the wizard's clothes continued to smolder. His body disappeared into the mist as Tori raised her bow and rained arrows down upon the beast.

Three horses of the Four Hooves galloped around the dead bodies of their friends. Slowly, the bodies began to rise and shake death from their fur, limbs, and armor. Leopards, cougars, wolves, humans, dogs, horses, cats and other creatures stood up and grabbed weapons or bared their claws and fangs.

They massed around the cougar, and he hissed dangerously at them all. He was as cold and slippery as a snake. The three horses galloped back to Red, Annie, Flame, and Louise as their army formed a circle around the Cougar. Tori unleashed another flurry of arrows, each flying into his bloody hide. He growled and started to form another fireball.

This time Red didn't waste a moment as Annie nudged her forward. Taking the sword of light, Annie rammed it into the center of the ball. It exploded and threw them backwards. The scent of singed hair and fur reached their noses, and they snorted and gagged at the smell. The four horses watched the beast pound at the ground with his mighty paws, trying to conjure enough shockwaves to create an earthquake. But they stood firm. Slowly, and methodically, they cornered Him. Annie, Red and the three ghost horses glowed with their own special light, the power flowing through their veins and into their very souls.

Now, now, now ... Annie felt her body say it, sensing every vibration in the air, every movement the beast made. Red pawed the ground, sending dust into small clouds.

Now, now, now, now ... Red seemed to say it, too. Their hearts merged into one rhythm.

Thrum, thrum, thrum, thrum, thrum, thrum, thrum...

Now, now, now, now...

Thrum, now. Thrum, now. Thrum, now. Thrum, now!

"Now!" they yelled in unison. They charged and Annie raised her diamond sword, deadly thin and white. Lightning made it glimmer like a thousand ice shards. The newly awakened army charged in too, each one plowing into the Cougar of Darkness. As the beast growled in anger, Red, Annie, the Bay, the Grey, and the White sliced open his chest.

"Nooooo!"

Then he vanished. It was over. He was gone; just like that.

On the breeze that blew through the crowd every one could have sworn to hear a voice say, "This is not over yet, my girl. Revenge will come and it will be sweet. You *will* fall then..."

Chapter 14

The darkness was overwhelming, but it really didn't bother him. He lived in it; he was a part of it. It was his home. The air was damp, yet scorching hot. The humidity made it feel like a twenty-pound weight was on his chest. No one else could ever feel truly comfortable in this place but him. It smelled of waste, blood, acid, and death. The odor was thick, like an incessant fog clogging his nose and blocking his senses. The Cougar shook his head.

A golden light could be seen in the distance, and he knew who it was. He didn't feel like being an enthusiastic welcoming committee of one. Thunder rumbled in the sky and golden light filled the darkness. A horse stood in front of Him, but the Cougar didn't cringe in fear.

"You filthy beast!" Sunrise spat and reared, showing his true power.

"You threaten my world and intend to destroy me? You're nothing now, and I curse you! I command that you live in darkness the rest of your days, which I hope is a long time. You will weaken and only one with a truly evil heart will be able to free you. Light! Vanish!"

The horse disappeared in a wink, or at least he thought it did, because the golden light had extinguished quickly. The Cougar growled and vibrations rumbled through his throat, into the ground. His rage over his defeat was building. Each day he gathered every ounce of magic and strength to plot his revenge. He would be patient and when the One came to free him of his prison, he would be ready.

"Yes," he smirked, baring his gleaming bloodstained fangs, "Oh, yes. I'll be ready."

———

Annie opened her eyes. She was lying on a bed of straw, covered by an old fleece blanket. The sun was rising over the eastern mountains, and the world was bathed in gold and black. Rising up into a sitting position, she looked around her and saw bloodied wolf resting fitfully by her side. An eagle lay with its injured wings spread out across the large room. A young leopard and cougar lay in separate beds of straw across the room. Annie reached out to pet the wolf's muzzle and felt a tingling in her fingers. *What's going on here?*

Her world began to fade and her heartbeat merged with that of the wolf. Darkness overcame her; darkness like the inky black found in the deepest cave. Walking slowly at first, Annie's feet felt like they had a mind of their own. She couldn't control them. A bright light appeared and its brilliance flashed through the blackness. She saw the most beautiful place she had ever seen. Yellow flowers with purple stripes glittered in the sun and yellow, red, and tangerine roses bloomed in a sea of color. Up on a hill she saw an emerald castle glistening before the sea. She picked one particularly beautiful blue flower and again felt the tingling in her hand.

Walking back toward the way she had come, her feet were in control once again. Annie found herself back in darkness, but this time she didn't mind. Something was drawing her, calling her. Then she saw it. The injured wolf was lying on his side and she could hear his rasping. She was glowing again and a realization went through her. *Am I becoming a healer?* Instinctively, she put the flower on his shoulder, stepped back, and walked away.

———

When she woke she found herself lying down with her hand on the wolf's chest. Annie checked his breathing and saw it was easier for him. Feeling hopeful, she went and checked on all of the other animals in the room. After a few minutes, visiting each one, she saw that they too were starting to recover. The room was filled with the scent of flowers. Looking over her patients one last time, Annie limped to the doorway.

It was then that she realized two things. The first was that she hurt all over; her right arm throbbed where she was stabbed and her legs and back stung from every fall and blow she encountered. Her eyes were blurry with tiredness. The second thing she realized was that she was in a castle. She stepped out of her room into a stone hallway adorned with colorful stained-glass windows. Flowers and plants were sitting on windowsills, and a long red carpet covered most of the stone floor. At the end of the hallway were two doors. One went up into the towers and the other went down into a basement, each lit by torches.

Annie climbed down the brightly lit staircase. At the bottom she became confused. Many rooms led to other rooms, some dead ends. It was an unending maze. A leopard guard stood next to the staircase, and she turned to him.

"Excuse me, how do I get to the courtyard? I'm Annie and I'm looking for my sister and my friends."

"Oh! Forgive me your highness," the leopard said as he made a clumsy attempt to bow. "I am so glad you are well! Everyone will be joyous to see you. Your highness's sister is out battle training with her steed. Allow me to escort you."

They walked past many more rooms before Annie spoke again.

"I'm curious, why are you calling me 'Your Highness'?"

"Oh! Does her majesty not remember? You are our queen, as the wizard has prophesied.

Annie then remembered sitting in front of the magic fire; it was there that Tori's father said that she was the true successor to the throne. She then remembered him smoldering on the hill, and his body disappearing.

"I've been here for a month or more and have never been told what this world is called. Would you tell me its name?"

"Oh, I'm sorry to disappoint you, Your Highness, but this world has no name. No one has bothered to give it one. Maybe that could be something you could remedy?"

They reached a large wooden door that had a large handle. The guard stepped back and said, "I'm sorry, I'm not allowed to go any further. It is not permitted."

"That's fine. Thank you very much, um, your name?"

"Fire Forest, my lady. It's the name of an old warrior from long ago. They even say I look like him." The guard posed proudly.

"I'm sure you do! Thank you very much Fire Forest."

He bowed once again as she stepped through the door and into a courtyard. The sun was shining and the plants glowed a brilliant green. She wasn't eight anymore, because yesterday was her birthday.

Feeling grown up, and older beyond her years, Annie lifted her chin and walked proudly out onto the huge courtyard. It was divided into four sections. One section had water fountains and statues. The second had a lovely garden full of plants; it looked very peaceful to her. The third was the main courtyard and gathering place. The fourth was the training ground that led off to a broken-down stable.

Walking swiftly toward the forth section, Annie saw Louise sitting astride the black mare. A knight on horseback was teaching her how to joust. From the stable, Red heard Annie approach and whinnied with happiness.

"Red!" Annie ran to her and hugged her neck. A stable man raced to place a saddle on Red's back for her and was about to put on the bridle when Annie said, "I don't want a bridle. Thank you, though."

He bowed and ran off.

Red looked offended.

"How could that human possibly think that *I'd* need a bridle?"

"Calm down, he's just doing his job. Normally people ride with bridles."

"So, Your Majesty, how does it feel to be queen?"

"Actually, it hasn't sunk in yet. Its definitely an unusual birthday gift!"

"So that means you're nine? Happy Birthday!"

"Thank you. Red, there's something I need to tell you."

"What?"

"I think I'm a healer, like you."

"I know. I saw the power enter you. You can heal and you can defeat shadows by yourself now—even without your sword. It's a wonderful thing."

"Sometimes I think I'd rather be on your back fighting shadows. It was much more exciting than watching the flowers grow. How long have I been recuperating?"

"It's been over a month since your ordeal." Red paused. "Well then, if you're up to it, let's ride and go find some trouble!"

Annie was about to mount when she saw an engraved name on her saddle: QUEEN ANNIE.

"They engraved my name on the saddle!" she cried with happiness.

Red laughed as she got on and they galloped toward a cart that held many long, wooden bars. Annie grabbed hold of one and held it in both hands. With a sneaky grin, they walked silently toward Louise and nudged her from behind.

"Hey!" Louise squealed. "That's cheating! I don't know how to fight *one* opponent, forget about *two*."

The girls pretended to fight each other for about ten minutes before Annie had Louise pinned.

"Got you." Annie gloated.

"Darn it!" Louise smiled in defeat. Annie, I love you. I'm so glad you are your old self again!"

"I love you too, sis." Annie smiled, sitting on Red, who was also grinning a horsy grin.

"Your Majesty, Annie? A leopard ran up to her, making an honest attempt at a bow as he spoke. "The three wounded monarchs—

Lead Wolf, Eagle King, and Leopard Flame-Pelt—request your presence in the Great Hall."

The leopards stayed? Annie wondered if they were now permanent members of the royal guard. Red seemed to have the same question, for she whispered under her breath, "They say the leopards are some of the most loyal creatures on this planet. I guess you earned their trust!"

"I hope so," Annie said as she looked up at the palace. The bright stonework gleamed against the sun. Three of the four watch towers were now complete. A few soldiers were working on the fourth, and animal allies were keeping watch for any sign of the enemy. Suddenly remembering the leopard's request, Annie answered, "We'll be there right away!"

Nudging her heels against Red's flank, Annie galloped off behind the guard, with Louise in hot pursuit.

Entering the doorway, Annie dismounted and walked along Red's side through the many rooms and corridors. The leopard led the way as if he had been born in the palace.

They reached a large room with windows on the west, north, and east sides of the walls. At the south end were two thrones, formerly belonging to the old king and queen. The largest throne had been redone to look more queen-like, with pillows and tassels and pastel colors. The sun was reaching the highest point in the sky and the light made the stained glass windows glitter like the flowers in the Healing Field. Roses, lilies, violets and other beautiful plants grew in pots everywhere.

Besides the three guests, the room was filled with leopards, wolves, eagles, knights, and noble townspeople. In the center of the crowd, three figures stood tall. One was the Great Leopard Flame-Pelt the Third, the second was the Lead Wolf of the Mountains, and the third was the Golden Eagle of Talon Peak. Louise caught up to Annie and together they walked into the room to greet their guests.

Annie felt embarrassed that, though clean, she was still wearing the same clothes she wore since first leaving Arfag. They were a couple feet away from the monarchs and Annie could see how truly horrible they looked, apart from Flame-Pelt. The wolf looked broken, his breath raspy. The eagle's wings were drooped and lifeless. They managed to look regal, however, in spite of their disabilities. The three bowed their heads and the two girls did the same.

"People of this world we call home," the leopard announced, his strong, deep voice echoing around the Great Hall. "You see before you today our leader, our new queen."

The crowd cheered, "Long live the queen! Long live the queen!"

The wolf spoke next and said, "She fought for your safety and freedom, and brought you a chance to live a happier life."

Then it was the eagle's turn to speak. "Sit upon your throne, Your Highness, and become the true ruler of our world."

The three animals stepped aside and Annie walked up the four steps leading to her throne. She sat as royally as she could, considering her attire. Flame-Pelt walked forward and placed a gold and green sash around her shoulders. Red walked up next and placed a gold and red tiara on her head. Everyone in the crowd bowed down before her, even Louise.

"Thanks Red," she whispered.

Red's eyes sparkled with amusement and she whispered back, "You're welcome, *Your Highness.*"

Annie almost burst out laughing as Red backed away.

The leopard king remained and said, "Your Highness, please rise."

Annie beamed brightly as she stood. Placing her small hand in the big cat's paw, the queen smiled even brighter as the leopard continued his speech.

"Before you today I give you not Annie, but a queen with no proper name. From now she will be addressed by a new name. From the home of the Leopard and the Fire of their souls, the queen shall now be known as Forest-Soul."

Louise gazed upon her sister. *Forest-Soul. It fits her nicely*, she thought. The crowd cheered, appearing to feel a little more confident having a queen with the name of a leopard.

They began to sing her name until Red walked up.

She looked at the mare questionably.

"What are you doing?" she whispered.

"You're a healer, and these people should know that," Red whispered.

Addressing the gathering of people and animals, Red began. "You all know who I am. I am Red Mare of the Four Hooves. I represent Joy and Healing. You know that a special power runs in my veins, and that power is to heal. During the battle, something wonderful happened. Sunrise poured power into your young queen. She is not only Queen Forest-Soul, but Queen Annie, the Healer." Red said the word "healer" so loud that the word echoed off of the castle walls.

To the crowd, having a queen with the power to heal was quite exceptional. They started cheering, "Queen Forest-Soul! Queen Annie the Healer! They chanted her names over and over. The cheers rang out through the halls of the palace and seemed to echo in the chambers long after the crowds had gone away.

Annie's chamber was adorned more or less like a humble villager's room. It was green, with green blankets, green and white pillows and wooden dressers. From the two large windows, she watched everything going on in the courtyard. Tori had been missing since the end of the battle, and Annie was starting to worry. Sooner or later they would have to return home, and she didn't want to leave without saying goodbye.

The moon was rising, and the training guards and knights filed into the stable and armory to put the horses and training gear away. Many torches and candles lit her room. She refused to have a fireplace and insisted that a guard or an animal deserved it more.

It was hard getting used to the fact that she was a queen. Not a princess, not a town hero, but a q*ueen.*

Annie bathed and got into a battle dress with a dark blue cape. The style of the battle dresses was more to her liking. You could run, ride, swim, do whatever you wanted to in it and still look good. She saw that her wardrobe had already been filled with more of the same dresses in a couple of different colors, but most of her clothes were red and gold. It was if everyone thought they were her favorite colors!

She left her room and slowly walked through the hallways. She decided she wasn't going to disturb Louise; her sister needed her rest. Instead, Annie decided to visit the courtyard where Red and Flame were keeping watch.

Her boots made a small clip-clopping sound as she walked with a long stride over the cobblestones. Flame and Red both snorted a greeting, and Annie climbed onto Red's back. As she sat there on the back of her friend, troubling thoughts came to her about Canyon, home, herself, her sister, protecting Arfag. She dreaded facing her parents when she went home. All of this worry was causing turmoil in her heart and head.

"So, you do realize you have to go home?" asked Red, reading her mind, as usual.

"Yes, I guess I'm just afraid of the future. Where is Tori? I need to go over a few things with her before I go."

"I haven't seen her since the battle," Red replied.

Flame pawed the ground. "Red, if you want to look for her, I'll guard the palace in your absence."

Red nodded her thanks and soon the girl and her horse set out to look for Tori.

The moon was rising, lighting the sky with a ghostly light. The mare and queen rode silently, gliding without wings across the ground. The small farm huts were dark masses of shapes before them, and it took them a while to figure out which one belonged to Tori.

"Red, do you think she'll be home?"

"It's worth checking, don't you think?"

The half collapsed shape of the old barn revealed that they had arrived at the old wizard's land. They peeked into the stable and saw the two horses, Lone One and Star. The horses snorted in greeting and pawed at the ground impatiently.

"Speak," Red Mare commanded. The wordless hellos quickly become voices.

"What are you two doing here?" Star asked almost accusingly.

"We're here to check on Tori." Annie replied.

"*What nerve!*" whinnied Lone One. "She's distraught over the death of her father, and you expect her to entertain you two? If I'm not mistaken, she said it was your fault her father died!"

"Our fault? She chose to battle with us, as did her father!" Annie said defensively.

"Easy, Annie, let's go talk to Tori ourselves," Red replied calmly. To the horses she said, "I'll let it go this time, but from now on, you will show respect to your queen when you address her!"

Red sniffed and they both walked out of the stable. The night air was cold and fresh, and the scent of flowers and old hay lay thickly around them. Even the faint scent of blood remained.

With no reply to their knocking, they entered the unlocked door of the hut. It was dark inside.

"Tori?" Annie whispered tentatively. "Tori?"

Silence. It was too dark to see if anyone was home.

Finally, a muffled cry and whine came out of the darkness.

"What do you want?"

"To help. We miss you."

"How can you *possibly* help me after what happened? The others were brought back to life. Why not my father?"

Red replied, "His body disappeared, Tori. How do you know he is truly gone?"

"I haven't felt his presence. He would have contacted me by now!" Tori moaned.

"Don't give up hope! Annie comforted. *Tori had lost so much*! *First her brother, then her bird, and now ...* "We want to give you a new home, to provide a better place to stay for you and your horses," Annie continued. "We want to announce you as heir to the throne when we are gone."

"Heir?"

"Yes, we have no one other than you who we can trust—no one who is truly ready to keep the kingdom in order until we return."

A light from a candle suddenly flickered, and they saw Tori sitting on the loft with a tear stained face and a confused expression.

"You're leaving? When? Why?"

Annie laughed a somber chuckle. "We didn't come from this world, Tori; you know that. We have to go back sooner or later. I just hope fate will allow us to return someday. So, will you do it?"

"Yes, I will accept the honor you have bestowed on me. Thank you."

They hugged each other and Queen Forest-Soul was pleased knowing that the kingdom would be in good hands.

Morning came faster than an arrow. Annie lay in her bed, tired from the night before. Her window let in a whole lot of morning light and it brightened her room pleasantly.

"Uhhh...." she grumbled and stood up. Every muscle ached. Even her hair hurt. After changing into her green battle dress, she glided down the stairs and into the almost repaired kitchen. The cook—an old, humped-over woman—handed her a small bowl of leftover vegetable soup.

"Something warm is always good for the soul," she advised. "You look like you're in a hurry Your Highness."

Nodding and flashing a smile, Annie dashed out the door, sipping soup as she ran. "Thank you!" she said.

Though the sun was bright and blinding, the air was still cold. It was as if some barrier in the sky prevented the warmth from getting to the earth. Tori, Lone One, Mystery the Brown Mare, and Louise were all standing in the cold courtyard, battle training. Annie was happy to see that they were trying not to use the reins. You shouldn't have to think about holding on to a set of reins or bridle during a battle. You'd best be served holding a sword and shield!

Wanting to test her theory, she shouted, "All riders remove your bridal. Train without them for awhile."

Although they looked uncertain for several seconds, the riders removed the tack from the horses' heads. At first they felt off-balance, feeling robbed of the one thing that offers possible protection. After a few minutes of practice, however, Tori and Louise were using moves that were a considerable improvement.

Satisfied, the queen ran up to Red Mare. "It's working!" she cried. "They can control their horses with their legs, and fight with both hands."

"I'm glad. For a while I thought I was doomed to wearing one of those things all the time. The saddle is enough of a burden!" Red shook her head and watched the training a while longer before proclaiming, "Who challenges Annie and I?"

Louise stopped working on her lesson. "I will!" she shouted.

Mounting quickly, Annie grabbed a wooden practicing plank. "Let's show her how a *real* warrior fights."

Red whispered back, "Let's go!"

The sisters stood facing each other. Louise was on her brown mare and Annie the Healer was on her mare, as red as the desert sun. Mystery and Red snorted playfully before charging. The younger sister was caught off-guard. Annie hit her with her wooden weapon and made her off balance. Louise mumbled something as she tried to regain her seat, yanking on Mystery's mane. Annie rushed at her again, and this time almost knocked her clear out of the saddle.

"What, the..." Louise reached for the saddle horn but missed and tumbled off the back of her horse. At first Annie and Red were worried she was hurt - until Louise's laughing filled the courtyard.

Wiping off her bottom, she grinned and proclaimed, "The only thing hurt is my pride!"

———

For a week they battle trained and they helped repair the town. One day after the first frost, when the sun was unusually bright, Red looked to the sky. She sensed something was coming. The bright orb glowed white-yellow as it made its way to the center of the sky. Red had been out all morning and knew Annie would be looking for her. Sure enough, shouts and hoof-beats came from behind. Looking down the hill she saw Annie upon Flame, Louise upon Mystery and Tori upon Lone One. A couple of mounted guards were playfully in pursuit. Loving the feeling of giving chase, Red made sure they were close enough to see her before galloping off. She felt drawn to the same forest that she had entered with Annie and a pang of sadness filled her.

Is this why I'm drawn here? So Annie can leave?

The mare wanted to stop running and return home but her legs wouldn't allow it. She led them deeper into the woods and came to a large clearing, big enough to have a small battle in its center. Red stopped in surprise.

There stood Sunrise, glowing in the golden-pink hues of a rising sun. He nodded his head slowly in greeting and the mare did the same. "It is time," Sunrise said softly.

Red's body sagged in disappointment. "Will they ever return?" The question tugged at her heart, hoping and not hoping that he would answer.

"That is for time to tell," Sunrise responded.

"Red!" Annie galloped into the clearing and stopped when she saw Sunrise. As the noble stallion looked at her, she bowed slightly in her saddle. Flame did the same. The rest of the group was dumbstruck by his beauty. Louise gasped at the sight of him.

A small, white circle of light appeared to his right. Slowly, it grew into a large portal.

"Is it time to go?" Annie whispered, tears forming in her eyes.

"What do you mean?" a guard asked, not understanding.

"We must leave now, but we plan to return again someday and rule again in peace."

Louise said nothing. She just stared at the portal, excited but fearful.

A young page spoke, "Who will rule until you return?"

Then to their surprise, a small word exited the queen's mouth. "Tori."

"We will ensure it." Sunrise's deep, church-bell voice boomed as he looked at the young sisters and then at Red.

"Say your goodbyes, girls," he instructed. "It is time to go."

Dismounting sadly, Annie turned to Flame first, and hugged his red neck. He nuzzled her in the shoulder and whispered, "Hey, don't worry; we'll be fine, and you'll be back. We'll see each other again."

Nodding she then turned to the guards. "I will return. I don't know when, but I *will* return. Take care of my friends in our absence."

They bowed low and said "Yes, my queen."

Turning to Red, Annie ran and hugged her tight around the neck, staining the mare's desert-red hair dark with tears. "Thank you, Red. You helped me get my sister back, and during the journey, you became my best friend. I'll miss you!"

"And I you, Annie. Someday, when the sun sets on a night of no moon, you'll return. Until that happens, I'll be waiting. But now Queen Forest-Soul, Annie the Healer, pull yourself together! You are a queen, and I expect you to act that way! No tears!" The girl straightened and sniffled quietly as the mare finished her sentence in a whisper, "And you'll still be my best friend also."

After Louise finished her goodbyes, the two girls stepped in front of the portal. They looked at all the faces they had come to love. Red, Tori, Lone One, Mystery, and the guards. They thought of their beloved friends in Arfag. They had come to think of this place as their *real* home. Their eyes glittery with tears, they each raised their right hand to wave goodbye. Their faces were solemn as Sunrise turned to them.

"In the snow turned pink from the setting sun, when the trees become shadows, find my name in the sky and the portal will open to you."

Once more the girls waved goodbye, then stepped through the white sphere.

The group they left behind mourned, as their queen and friend disappeared from their world.

Epilogue

The room was dark and menacing, hardly any life at all buzzed through it. The older girl realized it was the same time of the night when she had left this world upon Red Mare. Her sister Louise was sleeping and was, once again, five years old.

Annie found her red horse figurine on the bedside table. Its hooves were grass stained. Her book, *The Misty Garden Horses*, lay open on her bed. Quietly walking over to the shelf, she grabbed a pen and a giant stack of paper. Annie set the parchment down on her bed, preparing to write.

Louise woke up feeling depressed. "Mom and dad didn't come looking for us, did they?"

"No. But don't be too hard on them. They assumed we were playing tricks on them. When we didn't return, they got very worried and had the State Troopers looking for us all over the Susitna and Matanuska Valleys."

"What did Sunrise mean when he said, "Find my name in the sky and the portal will open to you"?

"It means when the time is right, the portal will reappear."

"What about the 'Find my name in the sky' part?"

"It means we'll see his name in the sky maybe in a constellation or the clouds or something. I really don't know."

Changing the subject, Louise asked, "What are you doing with that paper?"

"I'm going to write our story."

"Oh, really?" The young girl ran over to her sister's bed and sat beside her. "What's it going to be about?"

"About all that we just went through; our journey to a world that we don't even have a name for."

"About Red Mare and the Four Hooves?" Louise asked excitedly.

"Yes, and all our journeys and perils. We will write our book and then see about maybe publishing it. Or would you rather we just keep it a secret document between ourselves?"

"I prefer sharing it with the world!" Louise exclaimed.

"Me too." Annie looked up at the sky through the open window and said again softly, "Me too."

Together they wrote into the night, sharing every adventure, not forgetting any detail. Come morning they still kept at it, listening to the calls of flocks of geese flying south. Their parents, happy to have them home, were indulgent and brought food to the room. They stayed up late again the next night before finally finishing the last battle scene.

The book ended up being a hundred pages long, and they bound the pages together with glue and twine. The girls attached two pieces of white cardboard to the front and back of the book. On the front, Annie painted a picture of a horse as red as the desert sun. The mare was standing on a snowy slope with ghost-like shapes of wolves and cougars behind her. For the title they called it *The Four Hooves: Book one, Joy*.

Sitting back on the bed, they both let out a great sigh of satisfaction. They finally finished the first account of their story; a story that would keep on going as long as the great horse Sunrise ruled, and Red led the Four Hooves.

"Let's read it!" suggested Louise.

Nodding, Annie opened the cover and began reading the first page aloud. Suddenly they heard a whinny and looked out the window. They weren't certain, but they could swear that they saw a red mare galloping around the forest's edge. It was waiting and watching and then, gradually disappeared. Was it just wishful thinking, they wondered? They didn't think to look up at the sky. But if they had, they would have seen the northern lights dance like shimmering ribbons across the heavens and that some stars were connecting their light together to form one word: **Return**.